Mama Bear of Foster Care

#momof5

Adoption Day: Waiting at the Starting Line

Waiting for the judge to announce his final decision on our adoption was much like bracing yourself on the starting line of a race. I've been ready for so long, having been in training for years for this moment. I am focused and the adrenaline is surging through my veins. I am confident. I am ready. Looking at the others lined up next to me, I have my husband by my side, and we are surrounded by our kids. Three of them we have brought into this world ourselves, and two who were raised by someone else, and we get to be the ones that help them the rest of the way. They are all excited and see the great things in store from them as we run this race. We are a team, and will finish this race together.

On this day, June 25th 2018, I am vowing legally before a judge and my family that I will take care of these children for the rest of my life. Even as I can say fearlessly and confidently that this is what I want, I still have the fears that all parents do regarding their children growing up. Several thoughts creep into my mind.

1. What if they never love me as a mother?
2. What if we don't always have the financial money to support this new large family? I can't personally put each child through college and buy them a house. What if they aren't able to go to college because I can't support that financially? That would feel like a failure on my part.
3. Are people looking closer at me? Do they look harder for faults? Is someone going to say we are just using the system for gain? Well maybe I have. I am gaining two amazing children who I will love for the rest of their lives, but who says that's a bad thing. Yes, our goals turned quickly from fostering into adoption once I met them, but the girls melted my heart pretty instantly.
4. Will someone see me do something hastily or stupid once and decide I am unfit and call to make a report? Would the biological family do that to me to get revenge? My adopted and biological children would all be affected.
5. What if, in a future heated argument, one of the kids runs away? Or they end up in prison because I didn't do good enough? Or they spread lies about me? What if it doesn't turn out all right?

But…even though these thoughts flash through my head at the last moment, I wouldn't do this if I only *thought* I could do it. I would only do this if I *knew* that I could handle this. 100%. They are great kids. They are *my* kids. I have also vowed to myself and my husband that I will do this, and do it well. I have zero doubt that I was meant to do this. A million things in my life had led me to this moment, waiting for the judge to make the final decision. I had been waiting for this moment to be official for too long now. These girls are already my family, seventh cousins even. They look like us, they laugh like us, and they are ~~hurt, scared~~, excited like us.

I look back at the friends and family sitting in the back of the courtroom. I see my parents sitting with my three youngest kids, all color coordinated and fresh from our pre-court photo shoot that we just did. There is more family too. New family to me. An aunt, uncle and two cousins that belong to my almost-adopted daughters. I see a friend, who has been a role model to my daughters, and was able to say things that I wasn't able to say to them myself. She is next to her husband, a police officer in our community and one of her daughters. I see CASA workers, who have volunteered with my girls and numerous people who have worked with us from the state. The caseworker is at the table to the left of us, sitting alongside the state attorney. One the far left side of the room we have the guardian ad litem, an attorney who works hard to fight for the welfare of the kids. Several personal friends were there who worked in the court system. The bailiff who goes to our church sat alongside another mentor of my daughters, both requesting to work this shift so they could be here to witness this event with us. If I close my eyes, I can imagine them all in the stands cheering us on. We are almost there.

I have been waiting on the starting line for too long now. I have been just waiting for the rest of my family to step up to the line with me. It wasn't as easy for some as it was for others. Some of my kids have been right there with me since day one. Even my husband had to rely on my faith at first until he found his own answer. My oldest daughter was the last to step up to it and decide that she could be adopted. She didn't know if she should until the last minute of the foster placement. Too much fear of the unknown. Fear of abandonment, of being ripped away-again. But I have been here, waiting for you. You don't know it yet, but we will run this race together. Not one person gets left behind, and we will run it in step with each other. We all matter, and each of us contributes to what makes us a team. Team Jade. We are going to be a family now.

Pulse racing. Smiles forming. Hearts stretching. I hear the countdown.

Three…Two…We've got this…One…

"The adoption is final!" the Judge announces. And we take off.

The Story of Me

My family

Learning a little about who I am and where I come from might help get you into the right mindset for this book. I come from a very strong family. We have a sense of who we are because of our family history and culture. We have always had a focus on family history, and can trace our lineage back as far as possible on both sides of my family. I came from a very religious background, and my whole family belongs to The Church of Jesus Christ of Latter-Day Saints. It is a part of our heritage. Our family tree can be seen easily and we are all connected. Having a family like mine is kind of like the movie My Big Fat Greek Wedding. Many of us live in the same state, and I have an abundance of aunts, uncles, grandparents, and it seems like hundreds of cousins, both 1st, 2nd and some 3rd cousins that I could name as well as their families that they have created. If we were all to gather at a reunion going back a few generations of everyone related, we would likely have hundreds to thousands of living relatives. This is a very typical scenario within my culture and religion. We are connected to so many people. We even do family trees online and were able to connect with my adopted daughters. They are related to me, and are my 7th cousins, and 10th cousins to Brandon. We brought them to Idaho for a funeral, and they were stunned to see how many family members we actually had. Even more shocked when I said that most people weren't even there.

Brandon's family is a little different. His mom passed away just a month before I met him. He has three siblings who I have met, and an aunt who I haven't. He may have grandparents who are alive, there is really no way to know. His dad is local, but I have not met him and he isn't a part of our story. Brandon's mom, Patricia, worked her whole life to educate and help her children grow into strong individuals. They were home schooled in a way that taught them how to run businesses and learn skills. He has successfully run bike shops, a bookstore, multiple bakeries just to name a few occupations. They successfully bred and raised horses. When she passed away from cancer, the family was already grown and soon went their separate ways. We don't know very much about his family history, so we focus on mine.

Growing up in Oregon

I grew up in Oregon and lived there until I was 16. I was right in between the coast and the mountains. I learned to ski with my dad on Mt. Hood and swim in freezing water on the coast of Seaside. I have strong connections to the Hillsboro area still, and when I visit the church from my childhood, I still have familiar friendly faces there. I stayed busy as a child through music. I played the piano, trombone and violin. I even got to travel to Portland weekly and be a part of the Metropolitan Youth Symphony. I also was involved in various activities, like after school sports where I actually learned to do the uneven bars in gymnastics. I took ballet and jazz dance classes, but quit when I realized that there were people watching me. Nope, can't have that happening. I also was a girl scout, and participated in 4-H. I had a paper route and helped clean my grandma's police supply store. My first and favorite job of all time was working at the Oregon Zoo. It became my second home, and I love to go back and visit anytime I find myself in Oregon. I used to take a bus to the train station and travel to Portland to go to the zoo when I was just 15. I was very involved in school and in church. I spent a lot of time playing in my backyard and swimming at the neighborhood pool.

My immediate family consisted of my mom and dad, Lana and Duane. I have two brothers, Sean who is four years older and Andy who is four years younger. I have a sister Mandie who is just two years younger than me. All of them have travelled the world to be missionaries for our church. Between Sean and Mandie's families we have three nieces and one nephew. We did have three foster kids in our family for about two years when we were growing up. We lived just a mile from my mom's parents, so I got to spend my childhood and most holidays with my grandparents. I remember how Grandma Terry could transform her house into a spooky place to be at Halloween, and then on Easter she would make it fancy with adorable bunny decorations. She put intense thought into everything she did to make sure everything was perfect. My grandpa would always sit me down on his lap while sitting on his cream colored La-z-boy chair. He would try to embarrass me and ask me which boys I liked. I always told him that there were no boys. We kept that up until the day that I eventually called to announce that there was in fact a wedding coming up, so there must be a boy after all.

Moving to California

I was sixteen when I had to leave my life in Oregon and move to Southern California. It was a hard adjustment. There were people that were part of my childhood that I didn't want to leave. I did well in school. I was in marching and jazz bands, and even got to travel to Canada and Hawaii with the bands. I did well in school and practically made applying for scholarships my part time job as a senior. The work paid off, and I was able to make it through my college degree with several scholarships and grants. I had two best friends at Fillmore High and they all shared my name. I was the minority in the school. Although there were many blonde students, I was one of the only ones that got into the "natural blonde" category, along with my sister. It is a Mexican farming town, and I loved the people there very much. I still love to visit the town of Fillmore and visit with the people in the church who still remember me. On my last trip I had barely opened the doors to the church before a sister came running out of the chapel to give us hugs.

Just as I finished the last two years of high school, my family ended up moving to Utah. I stayed in California to go to college at CSU Channel Islands. I worked at the library on campus and loved being among the books. I got to memorize the Dewey decimal system and helped start the church institute program on the campus. Most say that the campus was haunted. I have plenty of stories that may attempt to prove my point, but that is for another time. I met some dear friends that year who I have very fond memories with. I lived just about 40 minutes from my Nufer grandparents. I enjoyed the opportunity of being around them and even living with them a few times while we all transitioned in the next few years. Looking back, my great Grandma May passed away the same time that my future adopted daughter was being born, and we have recently also learned that they are distantly related.

Meeting my soulmate

The summer following my first year I went "home" to Utah for the summer. It was there that my mom had met a special friend, who was in the last months of her life, passing away from cancer. You guessed it, it was Patricia. My mom knew before I had any idea, that Patricia's youngest son would be a part of our family. Being the amazing matchmaker that she was, I got to meet Brandon on July 17th, ten years from the date that my foster sisters went home, and Andy's birthday. We were introduced at the church building down the street from where we ended up creating our home. A million little things had led to that moment. For example, if my parents had picked a different house they were looking at just a few minutes away from the one that they bought, they would have never met. Or if I hadn't been at church that Sunday afternoon, we likely wouldn't have crossed paths. We spent nearly every minute together for the next month before I had to go back to school in California. My brother Sean was having a wedding reception in Utah for friends to come to. I remember Brandon was playing guitar and singing in the living room. We had been hanging out just a couple of weeks when my grandma leaned over and whispered "I see why you fell in love with him". I was such a private person, that I wasn't ready to admit it to myself yet, but it was clear I was falling for him. It was hard to leave him. There must have been a hundred signs in my life shouting at me that I was meant to be with him, and I'm not one for needing signs and still I could see them clear as day. A week or so after meeting him, we went on a long walk and I mentioned that I was going to name my first kid Jade, and that I had decided on this when I was in the sixth grade. I even had kept the flyer from the Imperial Tombs of China exhibit that I had visited in Portland on a field trip. I had decided back then as a 12-year-old, that the name Jade would become a part of my story. He mentioned that he was in the market for a new last name, since his dad was not in the picture, his current name left no meaning for him. A few weeks later he had gone to the courthouse to officially change his last name to Jade.

    A million pieces of our puzzle were suddenly fitting into each other. He came to visit me in California, which also happened to be the exact place that he was born and spent his younger years raising horses in Ojai. He had planned on proposing on the hilltop under the stars in Ojai, an idea that I may have subliminally planted in his head. I picked him up from the airport and we were both as giddy as a kid on candy corn. I had planned a fun date in Valencia at a food court that had a giant Barnes and Noble, a 50's themed Johnny Rockets diner, a movie theater and the mall. There were lights strung up and music played in the courtyard with a Ben and Jerry's ice cream stand in the middle of it all. As we parked in the multiple story parking garage, we were getting out of the car. The energy and excitement was just bursting. He said he had a gift for me in the car and he wanted to see if I liked it. I told him of course I would like it, whatever it was. Then, as we got back into the car, which was parked right in front of a red brick wall, he pulled out a ring box and showed me the most beautiful diamond solitaire I had ever seen. "I wanted to know, will you marry me?" The only words that I could think of was "OK!" And that's how we got engaged. I'm sure we were just radiating, because our waiter at Johnny Rockets could tell that we had news just by watching us interact. He was so thrilled with us because he had also become recently engaged, that he even paid for our desserts that night.

    This was just two months after meeting each other. We spent the rest of the semester visiting each other by traveling on planes, trains and cars to spend every spare minute together. We lived about eight and a half hours driving from each other. I worked very hard in school and also very hard at texting him every chance we got. I was great at doing both. I worked on getting transferred to the college near him, and the following January I was one of the newest students walking the courtyards of Southern Utah University. We were married on Valentine's Day, in the St. George temple. We have been here ever since, growing our family. I got my psychology degree, and minored in music. The few jobs that I have had since graduating were all in helping with disabilities, child abuse prevention fields, as well as teaching music lessons and starting my own small catering business. I was a part of Big Brother Big Sister for about 6 years, which was another stepping stone for becoming a foster parent. We worked hard and are very involved in the community, church and neighborhoods. My family all moved away. I still have a lot of family in northern Utah, but my siblings have ventured further, like Chicago, Hawaii and Orlando. Thank goodness for group texting and Facebook.

My first daughter, Lyla Belle was born five years to the date and hour of her grandma passing away. I like to think that maybe before this life they were together. We chose the name Lyla from the movie August Rush. It was the mother's name, and she was a cello player. I decided to buy and learn the cello because of this. It also means 'dark princess', and we decided if she were to be born with dark hair, that would be her name. Sure enough, little Lyla was born with black hair and dark skin. "I know who the dad is…but who is the mom?" the doctor had said. I chose the name Belle, because it meant beautiful and brought up images of a southern Belle. It just happened to be a princess name, but she wasn't named after that specifically. More on that later. Lyla is very much like me the older she gets. She strives to be the best student and does every kind of craft. She also loves to write and has a big artistic heart. She is generous to everyone and welcomes foster kids with open arms. Lyla earns the most money of the kids and shows more responsibility than most kids her age. She plays the piano and the violin. She is kind and tries to include everyone around her. I have been teaching her about kindness and bullies since her first day of kindergarten. Recently as I am talking with all of the kids in the car, reminding them that if they have a bully issue, there are things they can do about it (that is part of my job, teaching kids all about keeping themselves safe). I hear her from the back of the SUV, "Mom, I've been wanting and waiting for a bully so that I practice these skills, but I haven't found one yet." Just keep waiting, I tell her. They will come sooner or later. She is just an incredible kid, I mean who says that!

Next came Stetson Ryder. Yes, Stetson, as in the cowboy hat. When I was pregnant with my second baby, I went to Virginia City with my family. We wandered through the stores on the boardwalk, and my Grandpa Terry, a cowboy type himself, started saying how much he liked the name Stetson. At first I thought it would be a crazy name for a baby, but seeing the Stetsons on the wall and knowing that they were known for their excellent quality, it started to make sense. I was then hoping that I was having a boy so I could save this memory with my grandpa and bring both his and Brandon's cowboyness into our family. The name Ryder just seemed to fit. I loved the name Rider Strong, who was the best friend on Boy Meets World, a show that formed my childhood. This was also about the time that the Disney movie Tangled came out, so people kept asking if he was named after Rider Flynn. Not really, but we just went with it. I think Stetson's name fits him well. He wants to be a cowboy when he grows up. Or a toy maker. He is very honorable, even at a young age. He is the first and last to give me hugs every night. Stetson has a very tender soul, and he loves to create schedules for who gets to tuck him in at night. "Mom, it's your second night in a row to tuck me in tonight. Dad's first turn will be tomorrow. I love you ten times more than anything you could ever say to me." When he was born, he was the boy version of Lyla. They looked very similar and he was the best baby I have ever seen. He was so good as a baby, that I was adjusted to being a new mom for the second time so fast, that I decided I needed new hobbies-thus the introduction to Jade Catering. I learned how to conquer one of my fears, stacking wedding cakes. I made hundreds of cakes in the next couple of years. Stetson excels in school and it above average in every subject. He quietly gets his work done at home so he can be the first one ready to play on electronics. I'm pretty sure he is going to be a video game designer or an engineer. I wish that every mom had a little Stetson of her own. He is one of my favorite parts of parenthood.

  Baby number three entered the mix at the end of 2015, in her own due time. She was to be born before Thanksgiving, so we had family come down to meet the baby and stay for the holiday, the only one absent was her. She wasn't even born in the correct month! December baby it is. Waiting for her gender was a very fun part of the pregnancy. Some people thought we were crazy, but I loved it. When she was born I swore my husband was joking when he said "She's a blondie!" It was no joke though, she came out with white hair and a red swollen face. She must have been grasping for any Irish gene she could get her fingers on. Adeline Aurora was her name. We borrowed the name Adeline from a movie that had come out earlier that year, and looking through our family history, we have found both Lyla and Adeline names. We could see her unique personality from day one. This girl was a genius sassy pants. She is very much like the Michelle character on the 90's tv show Full House. I wouldn't be surprised at all if she were to pursue acting. Her middle name Aurora would have been Lyla's if she had been born blonde. It comes from the Aurora Borealis, the northern lights. It also means the dawn, or beginning of light. We weren't searching for another Disney name, but Sleeping Beauty happens to be my husband's favorite movie. As it turns out, every kid in my sibling's families also happen to have Princess or Disney names, including Charlotte, Diana, Maximus (remember the horse in Tangled), Sofia (from Sofia the First), and Jasmine. So I would say that we didn't intentionally name them all after this pattern, but when our daughter who was getting ready to be adopted wanted to add a new middle name to fit in, she picked a Princess name too.

    Year later, when the time was just right, we found ourselves at the courthouse adopting my two daughters from foster care. Emma is a girl unique to herself. She just might be the most resilient kids in the world. She was 8 when she came to our home. She had taught herself to be a survivor. She was diagnosed with cancer when she was just three years old, and finally beat it when she was seven years old. She intensely loves her mom and family so much. She had a hard time understanding that she was in an environment that just wasn't safe for her.

Emma came to love our family very quickly, and the emotion was reciprocated instantly. She was very delayed in school and we have spent hundreds of hours guiding her and catching her up. It is a struggle for her to learn math and writing skills. Even as a fifth grader, we are still working on basic handwriting techniques. But she has come so far. She has the same teacher, Mrs. Clark that she had in the 1st grade, when she was going through her cancer and neglect stages of her life. She has been one of her first advocates for making sure she was safe. Emma has a huge heart and sees the good in everybody. She would play and dance and sing all day if she were allowed to. She will be the first one to give everyone a hug, even a stranger. She bounces through the school and everyone knows and loves her. She won an award in front of the whole school when she was in fourth grade because she showed I.R.O.N. (integrity, respect, ownership and now). I made a video talking about all of the way that she shows these, and she cried along with the rest of the school. She was so excited to be adopted, especially when she realized that she would be in a safe home, and still be able to have a relationship with her biological family. The middle name that she chose was Merida, because she was brave and honorable. Meeting the spectacular princess at Disneyworld was a highlight of our adoption. She told Emma she was very proud of all she had accomplished. Emma makes me proud every day.

The last, or first, or oldest, or newest-however you may view her, is Tabitha. It doesn't take long to see that she is incredible. She was the last to join the family, but is also the oldest of the clan. Transitioning into a foster and adoptive home was not so easy for her. We took every step cautiously and have created a great bond. She has had a very hard childhood, and has chosen to grow and progress in spite of everything that she has been put through. Her heart had been stomped on so many times, that walls were built up. Going through things that you would hope no child would go through, she also came out a fighter. Tabitha is very musical and is also an artist. She was not oblivious like Emma was about how she was raised. We try not to dwell on the past, and we have a blast in the present. It has been very fun watching her experience new things, like joining the high school pep band, being asked to be a motivational speaker, learning to overcome cruel bullying, going to water parks, Disney parks, and working on her fear of flying. She even has been going to dances and has taken a liking to cowboys, just as I had years ago. She is still growing and learning about herself. I can see things in her that she can't see yet, and she has a wonderful life in store. She also got her name from a tv show, Bewitched. When she was adopted, she added two middle names to her name, Ray, after her grandfather, and Jade- so now a part of each of us is in her. Tabitha works hard and is growing into a young adult faster than I am ready for. She is going to be a wonder in the world.

So that is my family. They each have a unique personality and add something different to our family. We laugh and travel. We design clothing and do artwork together. We paint on the walls and sing along to musicals at the top of our voices, or for the shy ones, with the voice volume turned down. Our family loves to try new things and everyday we look for adventures. My story is not ending, but I can't wait to see what we turn into. This is our family of seven. I am a #momoffive.

Jumping off of my Everest

I am at the top of the cliff not quite sure if I am ready for this jump. Am I prepared? I don't know. All I can do is to rely on the air and my parachute. You see, the parachute is all of your strengths that you already possess. It is your talents, gifts, knowledge, training, experiences, faith, friends, and bravery. You already have all you need to jump off of Everest. Gravity happens automatically. I *will* go down. If I don't use my parachute, then I will crash. What happens if I crash? It doesn't necessarily mean that I will die-but it could. If I crash I break into parts of me. My bones may shatter and my spirit is torn up. Sometimes we can recover quickly and bounce back up. Other times people never really seem to recover.

I see so many people crash too often. Why? Are they jumping from a cliff that is too high? Are they missing part of their parachute? Or could they just be falling from a smaller cliff and crash so many times without recovering and get frustrated because the average person would be able to coast down from that height with no repercussions. I see this in people and "friends" on social media. They jump from one disaster to another without recovering. They live in crisis mode all the time. I get tired just watching it from my own cliff. My approach is different. I stay on the cliff until I have my own knowledge that my parachute and tools will get me down in a Mary Poppins gliding-through-the-air style. I've always been that way. I had just enough adventure to see the potential of taking a running leap, but I know where my destination will be.

When I met Brandon, we ran up to the cliff hand in hand and we could use each other's parachutes to get us down. No fear, only unbridled excitement to start our adventure together. We were 100% sure of our faith and future to jump and start our journey. When we decided to start trying for kids, it took much longer than we had hoped for. We had just the two of us for five years. Our adventures included traveling the world (or at least a few very fun parts of it), getting my psychology degree, running a business and getting our home ready and in order for kids. It apparently wasn't our time to jump yet. We were ready, but the elements didn't work to our favor yet. Eventually things did line up. There was perfect weather, a good place to land, parachutes were stocked and ready to go. And we took three jumps like that off of the "kid mountain". We had plenty of people who were waiting at the bottom supporting us. Some gave excellent advice. Others threw us baby showers. We received gently used clothing to get us started from loving neighbors. Everyone around us was excited for us too. They were great supporters. Many have already taken the kid plunge themselves, and knowing fully what we would be expecting, were here to help us navigate and get down safely to the ground.

With your own kids you pretty much have complete control. You get to decide how many baths you give them and where to do them. Some parents chose to have the babies get bathed in the kitchen sink, and other times they have their own bath within the standard bathtub. As long as they get a bath, there doesn't seem to be a right or wrong way. You get to choose what and how you feed them. This is often a hotly debated topic among moms. Breastfed vs. formula fed babies are looked at differently in many mom groups. Just make sure they are fed! It is up to you how you dress them and what colors they are allowed to wear. Some moms I know insist that their baby girls are dressed in pink, and I also know some parents who insisted that their baby girl does NOT like to wear pink. The moms and dads get to ultimately decide how to raise their little ones, and as long as they have the basic needs, things are going to be alright. You get to choose if you sleep train them or how to adjust the car seats, or what toys they will use for stimulation. You may have many advice givers and maybe some who try to take your control away, but ultimately you are in charge. All of these jumps are from varying sized mountains, depending on how big of a jump this adventure is going to be for you. I jumped off of plenty giant mountains.

But..when did I notice that there was an Everest in the distance? I know a few people who have jumped off of "Everest" in the fostering community. There are those obvious ones. Some have had around a dozen children, many of them adopted. There are the moms that donate their lives for special needs kids. Or the parents who take in family even though they didn't offer or sign up for that. They have no real training or desire, but they are family and it is the only option if you want the kids to stay with family and not get sucked into the system.

Here is the thing about jumping off of Everest: we don't get to decide that Everest is the same for everyone. For some, jumping off Everest is having a child. It is the biggest jump that they will ever do, and maybe it's not going so well. Perhaps they have had to change or even leave their whole lifestyle for a child. Maybe they suffered a difficult pregnancy or even an unwanted one. Having a baby can really have the potential to be the hardest part of someone's life. For someone else, their jump could be getting through medical school and working five jobs just to survive while running a nonprofit and having a handful of children at the same time. There are really people that can handle that and that is their jump from Everest. For other people it will be just getting out of bed each day. I don't get to judge what your Everest is. Even though I can't judge your Everest jump, I am not going to be silent about my jump. I want to show others that maybe they can find a way to do a jump that they didn't think they could do.

    My Everest has a name. It's not motherhood, even though that was a HUGE jump in my life, I think I was trained adequately and I did that jump just like most people did. I wouldn't say it was getting an education either- I did that and loved every difficult excruciating sleep deprived moment. It's not living in poverty, because somehow I was blessed to have just enough to live a normal life. My Everest is called **foster care**. It is one jump that many people don't even think about taking. I'll tell you what, foster care Everest is far away from the regular jumping cliffs. It's a whole journey just to get to the base of the mountain. Looking up to the top is daunting because the top is in its own atmosphere. It is gloomy and dark with thunder. Are those bats!?! Possibly, but they probably won't bite... it's not very inviting. This is not a journey that most people are going to want to go on, and most don't end up completing. I had to go through the process multiple times just to finish getting licensed. You will learn that there are some gnarly cliffs to conquer on your way up the mountain. With names such as medical forms, therapy, home studies, licensors, auditors, reports, inspections etc. Why do we do it? Because at the top of the peak we see a face of someone who is waiting for us to help them jump. That's right, they can't jump without *our* parachutes. Tragedies will occur when they try to jump on their own. These are NOT hypothetical faces. There are real breathing, laughing, crying, numb people who need you. How long have they been waiting for someone to rescue them? These are children. Maybe you see a drug addicted baby. Or a sibling set of six. Possibly even an older teenager who has AIDS and a baby of her own. Maybe you even see neighbor kids that you care about. You never know who is waiting for you.

Generally, we don't know what is at the top, and you can't see them until you hit the peak. You don't have long to decide. There are not going to be dozens of kids that you get to pick and choose from. In fact, there may not be any at the moment. But you have made the journey spiritually, emotionally and physically. So, you are ready, even if they aren't. I have had kids placed in my family who did not want to be with us. Sometimes their level of trust and safety has just beat them to the ground. They have no more spark in their life and the light left their eyes long ago. They don't want to look at you or to know that you exist. This is not something to take offense about- in fact, they don't really even see you. When their own vision has been darkened, they rely on their survival mode. Too many traumas and abuses have engulfed their own lives. So when they slam doors on you, rub feces on the walls, run out of the house or break your special treasures, you don't take it personally. They just need to establish some sense of control, and sometimes this is the only way they know how to do it. They aren't aware of why they are doing this. All they know is that being ripped from their family or from whatever "home" that they had before you, and they are being thrown into your waiting arms. The arms of a complete stranger, is not how they want to go down.

There are those times though, when they do run up to you and call you mommy before you even get a chance to say your name. These kids are all worth it. Sometimes we get to see the rewards much quicker with the really excited and loving children. There are children that I have fostered, and one I even adopted, who are filled with so much love that it bursts out of them. They just love everyone and everything, and their worlds are filled greatly with visions of rainbows and unicorns. My daughter has truly changed the way that I see the world. She has added a whole dimension of myself that didn't exist before I met her. These are the kids that we secretly hope we will have placed with us every time. Still, no matter how much you have prepared for your flight down to the ground, you are never really ready to take the jump. It's a long way down.

So what is the jump about? You will see life from a new perspective. When your parachute is activated, then time is suspended and the soaring proceeds. What happens at the beginning of the fostering jump? You meet your new friend, and bring them home. This is a HUGE step. Sometimes foster parents go all out when they meet their newest family member. They may order five types of pizza, take them bowling, go buy new bedding, empty the whole bedroom and maybe even go buy a new bed set all on the first night. With my first call they asked me to go to the local children's respite center, which also happened to be my place of employment. I went into a classroom and sat down with a kid. No introduction, no representative from the state.

I didn't even know if he was the actual kid, and I don't think they told him that he was entering foster care and going home with a new family. It was so awkward!

He just played games and I waited with my two kids, keeping them entertained while trying not to be too obvious. I didn't want to say anything in case he didn't know he was coming home with me. I was just some random white lady who didn't match his ethnicity at all. Eventually the caseworker did show up after about 40 long minutes of waiting. He was sitting in my car within about 90 seconds. No paperwork was signed. I knew his first name and they told me to expect to keep him about five months. Then the car door closed. That was it? Where was my police escort home? Did he need a booster seat for my car? What school do I bring him to tomorrow? There was no call for the rest of the night. It was already past office hours and the caseworker was coming from a different emergency from the next town over. My drive home was surreal. I had someone else's kid in my car. Is this legal? When do they contact me again? The caseworker didn't give me her number. I helped him unpack into his new room.

He looked up after a while and asked, "When is dad coming home? Wait, is there a dad?" It is all so foreign on both sides. They say a foster kid coming into your home is kind of like traveling to a different country. The smells are odd, the food is cooked strangely, you even have to ask where the closest bathroom is. Yet they are supposed to feel like your own new kid, even if it is just temporary. Then they have to somehow shower, get into clean clothes, get their bed made and go to sleep. It's kind of like hosting a sleepover with a stranger. Do they need songs, extra water, to be tucked in? Depending on the age, they can't even talk yet to tell you what they need. I have rocked countless foster children to sleep, and it really is an odd feeling.

With your own children, it comes naturally to hug, kiss, swaddle and cuddle to sleep. Doing some of these things to a little stranger's baby feels anything but natural. You do it anyway. If they wake up from night terrors or drug withdrawals, they will take any love, simple connections and gentle touches anywhere they can get it. It is in these little moments when you remember the horrors of what was in their foster care files. I read of things that you hope only happen in horror movies. Closing your eyes and remembering that you read about the drug needles at their kitchen table or knowing that they slept in beds that dogs used as bathrooms, terrifies you. There are images that you haven't actually seen in person, but you can imagine it through their experiences. The alleged sexual assaults that could never be proven replay in their own heads as they sleep and we imagine our own version of what we have read, trying not to picture what they have gone through. Cringing when we do.

The babies shake because their bodies were just barely connected to their mom's food supply which could have contained powerful narcotics. Sometimes they just need their blankets or a special stuffed animal, but we just don't have any clue that a comfort object even exists for them. Maye the child just needs a sound machine or to smell the lavender shampoo that their mom used. What do we know? We know that night is the time when we are supposed to sleep. We like our sleep. We have grown accustomed to it. We expect to sleep after we make our first attempt at bedtime on the first night. As we lay our head on the pillow and take a deep breath, we begin to hear a soft whimpering, followed by loud crying. Then the screams start, and often continue throughout the night. They sometimes scream in their sleep and it happens every night. The terror coming from their rooms makes your heart beat faster. You vow to get to the bottom of the screaming, but sometimes you never find out the root of the problem because they end up getting placed back at home before you can get them the help that they need. Eventually, usually, they do fall asleep. As you lay your head down and close your eyes, you think: "I just earned $14.60 for all of that work today". That's probably more than you would pay a regular babysitter for your non-foster kids. Or how much it would cost to feed half of your family at Taco Bell. Or it may cover one of the fifteen shirts you need to buy them. Maybe that's what you would make for one hour of work for your job. You don't do it for the money, but you still end up having that thought the first night when you get a placement.

  You are still plummeting. Waiting for the parachute to open. We start again tomorrow. Progress is usually slow. Sometimes you get the honeymoon stage, other times you do not. It could take hours, or it could be months. People are shouting encouragement from afar. They see you but no one truly sees your view looking down from your Everest. Then it happens- never when you predict it, but it happens. Your parachute opens and you inhale for the first time, not realizing that you had been holding your breath. You get thrown back up near the top and for once get to see things again, but in slow motion this time. You can slow down and look around you for the first time. You notice things that you could have sworn weren't there the first time. You missed so much when you first jumped off, and everything had been so confusing. Now you are getting the hang of it (pun intended). The connections are finally being made in your family relationship. Things are finally starting to make sense of the behaviors you have been seeing. You now realize that you really do have the skills in your parachute that had been dormant. You can do this!

You are alone in the sense that you are seeing things through your own eyes. Hopefully your partner is still soaring right with you. Even though they are on the same journey as you, the connections you make will be slightly different. Communicate what you are seeing from up there. Figure out what is happening by talking about everything. You are alone in this, but in a way you aren't. You may have a whole family rooting for you. You have a caseworker watching every step you take. People from the system are frantically taking notes and analyzing it from their own perspective. They think that their perspective is always correct, and often don't take into account that we are the ones attached to the kids, risking our lives and our families, day in and day out. We see a hundred things that they can not possibly see. We are the ones holding onto the child.

When your parachute opened, you realized what strength you really do have. The trick is knowing which cliff to jump off of, and when to do it. These foster kids may have already used their parachute. The parachutes from the families that they came from were just not adequate for them. They might be missing some knowledge, or the addictions and unsafe behaviors don't let it open. Whether they love you or hate you, your parachute is what the kids need to survive. It will have to be strong enough for the whole family. If your parachute is not strong enough yet, then this is not the right mountain for you to be jumping from, or maybe it's not the right time yet. Strengthen your parachute before the jump, and when the time is right, hold on tight and take the running leap.

In the words of Erin Hanson:

> There is freedom waiting for you,
> on the breezes of the sky, and you ask,
> "What if I fall?".
> Oh, but my darling, what if you fly!

Sharing My Calm

"When little people are overwhelmed by big emotions, it is our job to share our calm, not join their chaos". -L.R. Knost

This phrase should be plastered in every foster parent's homes. These emotions that they experience are the leftovers that happen when they are faced with trauma. Everyone has trauma. Even before you are born you have some amount of trauma, and sometimes the trauma can actually rear its ugly face early in life. Just the process of being born and joining our world is traumatic. All kids will have some amount of childhood trauma. We can only hope it occurs from the medial things in life. I was stung by a bee at age 6 and it hurt and so I have learned to be more careful around bees. The end. That was one of the moments of trauma in my life, that I was able to learn from. Kids are bullied on busses, which can be traumatic even if no actual physical harm shows. Being lost at the grocery store can also be frightening. Having your parents divorce when you are young can leave scars. These are just a few basic examples, and have nothing to do with childhood trauma that the foster kids have to go through. One example of a more traumatic event is losing a direct family member to death or being abandoned. If not handled properly, These events can absolutely devastate a person, no matter what age they are. This is kind of the beginning of the trauma scale for most foster children.

 I call myself a "mama bear" of foster care, because I have made a mission of protecting foster kids, and guiding through the trials that they are bound to face. A typical case that gets handed over to foster care involves substance abuse, physical abuse and/or neglect. I had heard this during my pre-service training, but I thought that seemed to be too basic of a statement. It didn't take long to realize the reality of this statement, not only that, but usually they are all intertwined. How can you possibly gain an addiction to dangerous substances without alienating your parental duties, leading to neglect? I have seen kids miss about half of the days at school because the parents were too out of it to even get them to the school bus. Once the kids can get onto the bus, then the faith in the school system will kick in and they can take over for the next 6.5 hours. So many are easy to judge the school systems and lack of concern that the teachers and administration show for the kids. I find that to be the reality very rarely. Only once did I have a principal tell me that "his job is not to babysit the foster kid". That was a hard one to hear when I was already emotional and pregnant at the time. Or maybe I was pregnant and emotional-either way, it was a bad experience.

    The trauma that these kids experience at home is similar to what you would see in the movies or in your nightmares. I have the opportunity to go into the public schools in Southern Utah and teach the little kids about the different kinds of abuse. Of course, we have to be very gentle and word everything exactly politically correct. We teach that there are four main types of abuse. The definition of child abuse is anything to hurt or harm a child on purpose. The first is physical abuse, which is any kind of abuse that leaves a mark on their bodies. This could mean bruises, broken bones, scratches, burns or anything that you can physically see. Emotional abuse is when someone repeatedly puts you down or threatens you with the intent to cause emotional harm. Although it is kind of like an invisible abuse, the effects can last for the rest of your life. The next is sexual abuse, whether it is touching or non-touching, we cover it all. With the older kids we talk about how the internet, texting and phone apps can lure you into unsafe situations. We tell them that it is not their fault, and give them the tools to be able to report and stop the situation. This type of abuse is truly life altering. Neglect is the fourth abuse, and one that we don't always see. It's literally the absence of getting the basic needs in our lives met. I am very passionate about teaching the young kids what is abuse and what they can do to prevent it. But how sad is it that we have to go into the school to teach this? These are things that the parents should be talking to the kids about in the home. All of these abuses are extremely common in foster care, in fact I have had several kids who have suffered through every abuse on this checklist. If you are thinking this is unfair, you bet it is. It is despicable and disgusting the chaos that these kids have had to live with on a daily basis.

How do we train ourselves to be their calm? What do they get out of it?

We need to remember that children are going to have emotions. It is normal for them to express what they feel. It becomes our responsibility to teach them how to use those emotions and translate them into acceptable behaviors. I think that we often get too caught up in what is acceptable behavior that we forget to take a few seconds to remember that the way that our little ones are often actually very normal for kids their age. We have to be able to teach the little ones that although it is normal to have all kinds of emotions, all behaviors are not acceptable. Throwing objects on purpose to hurt another person is not going to be acceptable at any age.

One thing that I have noticed is that our emotions as parents can rise to the surface in just an instant. Too many times I have found myself getting fed up with the toddler who is screaming and kicking on the floor of the grocery store. When this situation arises, we often start to parent out of fear. We go more into a state of panic and urgency because we want to get the child in control as soon as possible. Do you ever think what you look like in times like these? Imagine another fellow shopper entering the isle just meandering through the store deciding what to make for dinner. They come across a person who is red in the face, eyes bulging and fists clenched. It is evident that they are clearly under the control of the two-year-old. The average person doesn't actually like to feel like this. They may feel ashamed that they got so overwhelmed or frustrated. For some, this is a daily or even an hourly event. This is the point when they need some parental intervention, which is totally possible to get on their own with a little self-care. For those parents who are not able to address these problems by themselves, outside intervention may be helpful, like what I do for my job. When we start parenting out of frustration, we are only teaching our kids how to act in the moment. We don't want to share our chaos. Just as we want to teach our kids to take control of their behaviors, we must teach ourselves the same principle. It's like the concept where you catch your child hitting someone, and in a moment of rage you slap them and yell WE DON'T HIT IN THIS FAMILY!!! Well...actually you do, and now you have taught them that it is ok to hit anyone else when they get frustrated. How much stronger would the message be if you were to calmly, with eye contact, let the child know that it hurts people physically and emotionally when they hit people. They respond so much better. It's a basic parenting skill. Parenting 101. Yet, sometimes we lose our temper and end up teaching the wrong things at the wrong time- and they always seem to learn from our example.

    Calm parenting is a great goal to have, it is one that I imagine we all wish we could improve on. When parents are in a neutral mood, it becomes so much easier for the kids to connect and learn what you are striving to teach them. We can have the best of intentions but still lose our cool if the kids know exactly which tactics will end up triggering us. Why do we lash out at the ones that we love the most? It is so easy to place the blame on our kids when they are being disrespectful or belligerent, but too much of this and then we can see ourselves getting defensive.

Parenting styles differ between every person. Some people may even try to put labels on their style. There is the *let them cry it out* parent, *a spanking never hurt anyone* parent, *bottle feeding vs. breastfeeding, cloth diapers vs. disposable, or how about the I don't let my kids eat red dye #5 because it will cause autism* parenting style. I don't think we are going to find many people who subscribe to one whole system of parenting. We are all individually shaped by our experiences and unique personalities. It is likely the childhood that we had experiences, which leads our brains to develop the principles and rules that we use to run our lives. We see this very commonly in the cycle of abuse. For example, Pete's great-great-grandma whipped her son, who beat his kid, then Pete's grandpa hit Pete's dad, who taught Pete that it was ok to use excessive force to discipline children. This does not imply of course that every person who was physically abused will abuse their own offspring. It also doesn't mean that someone who had had no history of this abuse will not be capable of abuse. Life and behavior is just not that simple, but the cycle of abuse can definitely be a factor when it comes to abusive family members.

Triggers

We also know that traumatic experiences in our lives can cause us to develop certain triggers. I have had several foster kids who have emotional triggers to smoking and alcohol. We are a strict no drugs and substances family, so we don't run into this situation all the time. Brandon and I were once catering a wedding and brought along our 13 year old foster daughter. We had a three-tiered aspen log designed wedding cake, along with gourmet salads, pastas, vegetable platters, pulled pork sandwiches and desserts. It was in the mountains in a beautiful location and the wedding was perfect. The trees were full of colorful leaves and the weather couldn't have been better if we had ordered it for that day. There was music and dancing the whole evening. We worked for about 4 hours at the venue sight in our high heels and fancy attire so we could match the atmosphere. My foster daughter was excited to be able to experience this time as an honorary caterer, but as soon as we were able to pack up and leave, she was the first one in the car. She had been a little silent the whole evening, but I figured it was just because her feet were blistering from the shoes. She opened up on our long 40-minute windy drive down the mountains and let us know why she had really been quiet. While my husband and I had been relishing the beautiful weather and fussing over every intricate detail of the night, she had been watching all of the guests consume alcohol. There were kids at the party and family had flown in from all over the country to attend this affair. There was the typical amount of alcohol that would have been expected at this type of event. By the end of the night, a few people had been dancing on the floor who we could label as tipsy, but nothing out of the ordinary.

    Her childhood experiences however, made her hyper-aware of any alcohol usage around her. She could name every guest who went to get another drink, and could even tell us what kind of drinks they were favoring. She had been with us for three months at that point and was still new and cautious to opening up to us. She spent the rest of the ride telling us why she had triggers to alcohol and cigarette smoke. No surprise, it was because of the experiences in her past that had scarred her. She talked of the parties that her mom would throw, and the scary company that she would invite into the house. The smells reminded her of the times in her life that she did not feel safe. From then on, we knew what some of the triggers were for her, and could help her get through the emotions that came with them, because we took the time to understand the behaviors. Fortunately for us, we live in a virtually alcohol and drug free world in our family.

Triggers can be caused by so many things. Certain smells, songs, tv shows, buildings, roads, people, movie plots (even Disney movies!), books, cars are just a few of the triggers we have dealt with. We have to be careful not to drive on certain streets in our town because we can see the panic in the kids eyes as they remember when they were assaulted there. Or maybe a movie which has a pretty standard plot where a character only has one parent, triggers them, throwing their abandonment issues in their faces. I have heard of a little girl being triggered by the sound of a popsicle wrapper opening, because in her past every time she heard that noise, she was about to be raped. We really never know the extent of the triggers, or how many we will run into. One thing that is a big trigger that we can't prevent is the season of the year. As you approach the anniversaries of children being removed from their parents, be prepared to watch for irregular behaviors. So many children are taken around the holidays, especially Christmas and New Year. I hear too many reports of family gatherings where there is alcohol involved, and domestic disputes result in new foster placements. When the holidays then come around the following year, anxiety shoots up and the behaviors will escalate, no matter how joyous and jolly you try to make the season. It is a reminder that they are not with their real families. The year mark of entering your home needs to be treated with respect. I have had children go off the deep end on these days, you see the anger, hatred, and the loss that resides within them. Love them anyway. You will get through it.

Birthdays are also common triggers. If the kids are actively having supervised visit with their biological family, I always try to schedule a visit as close to the special day as possible. I also tend to get a ton of presents, about the same as you would get for your own children. When we have siblings from the same family in our care, I also get them a gift too. One year we took the kids swimming and let the mom and grandma show up to give gifts and hugs. I decided to get them their own beach towels, just so they know they are being thought of too. It's hard for me to buy gifts for someone else's kids, I never know what to get them. I don't know what the norm is, but I have seen from personal experience that the kids usually just get one gift from their family. I always found that really interesting. I'm spending so much to make sure that their birthday is fun and memorable, and buy the whole toy aisle in hopes that I got something right and they won't be sad on the big day. Then the mom comes and brings one single toy. Maybe that's all they can afford, it just seems like they would have been thinking about this for a while had could have come up with a few options for the kids they know best. I'm not trying to judge, it's just a mystery I still need to learn about.

It seems that chaos comes from a lack of control. I can think of a few examples of parenting chaos. One is bringing the kids to public places exploding with crowds. Think of your last visit to a carnival or a zoo or a parade. The kids are easily lost, there are bathroom accidents, food dropped on the ground, babies crying and our ability to control is being tested. If we had complete control over the placement of bathrooms, and locations to sit, and the ability to have the children walk in a straight steady line, slowing down when we slow down, speeding up when we speed up, then we would see very little chaos. Another example of chaos is sickness. As much as we wish we could control it, there is a horrible experience that comes along with a child throwing up all over the place in the middle of the night. We lose control of the situations and chaos takes its place. Imagine the amount of chaos exists in a foster child's life. What they want is to be back home with their family…and at the root of it, what they *really* want is to be safe.

Even though we as functioning adults know that the child is safe placed with us, the child does not necessarily agree. They have no proof that your home will be any safer than the home with the family that they loved. No wonder they are living with dissonance inside of them. No wonder they are sad. No wonder they may act out to gain any semblance of control.

My opinion is that we need to slow down our parent minds before we talk too fast and treat the children as we would another adult. It is far too easy to start barking instructions the very second that the children walk in the door from school. Clean your room. Do your reading. Clean your room. Do your homework. Cleanup the tv room. Put your shoes away. The truth is, my foster kids can't handle that much nagging all at once. Your biological children shouldn't be able to either. We can handle it as adults, sure, but children need directions in smaller steps. The first thing that kids need when they hop off the bus, or bounce into your car in the pick up line is kind and caring expressions of love. I am working on this all the time, because my mind is racing after school to finish everything as quickly as I can. They need to know that you missed them and you are glad they are home now. Smile! Seriously, it makes a huge difference. Laugh with them. Give them hugs. Imagine what they must be picturing waiting for them when they come home if you are shouting orders at them everyday. Slow down your mind so you can get onto the same wavelength with them. Chances are, they will start telling you about their friends, and the crafts they made, and the games they played at recess. Maybe they will even tell you something more serious, but they won't feel capable of doing this if you are focused on your own agenda.

Try to find a good balance between drill sergeant giving orders to clean every little speck in their room, and a laid paid pushover. As much as we want their rooms clean and chores to be accomplished thoroughly, look at the task through their eyes with their own experience. It often works better to give them one task at a time, or else all of the commands that you gave them will become chaos in their minds. Why? Because they have lost control of the situation. I have a daughter that will spend two hours fighting with moans and groans while she completes five steps in her bedroom cleaning assignment. Another daughter however, will skip around singing and accomplish the task within ten minutes. The difference is the way their minds are wired, and how much chaos they can handle in their lives.

If we do it right, we are training these kids, whether they are permanent in your home or temporary, to have the life skills that they need to be able to be a successful adult. This is what I even explain to my kids when they are questioning why they have to go through the pain of chores from the bossy lady. As long as I have kids at home, this will always be something I need to work on. Tune into your kids, and listen to them. Don't raise your voice. No name calling. Join them in their chores and teach them that they are not a bad thing, just something that can help them learn responsibility in their lives. Don't teach them to whisper under their breath or to gossip. I don't want to join my kid's chaos, I want to be part of the calm steadiness in their lives. I want to be the example that they can look back on when they have kids of their own, of how to treat and teach their own kids. After all, the most important work that we do is in the walls of our own homes.

We have to be cautious. No matter how much we relive the movie in our heads that we think *may* have been what the kids went through, we can't really truly know their feelings. We might see some massive mood swings that they may not be able to explain. It will take along time for them to become regulated. Little phrases that we use can be misinterpreted by their chaos. The way that we correct little behaviors could leave any one of us in tears. Just because, like in a dating relationship which is new, we need to learn how to communicate. We may even need to learn how to fight. When I was young, I would sometimes burst into tears and tell my parents that they were yelling at me. I was just really sensitive and any form of escalation, I would interpret as 'my parents are mad at me'. It would drive my parents crazy. They would say:

"I'm not mad at you."

"Yes you are, I can tell."

"Well, now I'm *starting* to get mad!"

I do have one child that has received these same genes. Poor kid. No, we are not mad at you, just calm down. It can be like this with foster kids too. They may have so much fear or anger in them that little things are interpreted as something else instead. We just may not understand the perspective that we each have, at least until we understand how to communicate with each other. Some fostering relationships never end up working. Things can go horribly wrong and it can be out of our control. There will be some parents who set high expectations and kids who may pick up on that and see themselves as not good enough. Or maybe some of the older kids might have so much damage that they feel like their life is hopeless and their only option is to rebel. I have seen many younger kids who have too many disabilities for the parents to handle. Some conditions are very common in foster care such as anxiety, fetal alcohol syndrome, RAD, depression, autism, learning disabilities, speech problems and the list goes on and on. It takes special people to be able to willingly step up to the challenge. What if you end up adopting them and have to be their caretaker forever? It's a huge challenge to walk into. We are not all equipped the same way. We may lose control and we may fail.

There was a video shown to us in the foster care training of a girl who was very angry. She came from a very scary household and there was obviously domestic abuse, which she would hide her little sister from when the fighting started. She had to pack up her things in a garbage sack and move from one household to another. She didn't react well to the changes and was often very angry. She had been separated from her younger sister and the loneliness and anger was very telling on her face. She would start to feel comfortable in one home, then be removed and put in home after home. She ended up in a home with a mom who wanted her to feel comfortable. They started to create a routine. When things were feeling more comfortable, the foster mom gave her a shirt that she was thinking she would love, but it triggered some scary flashbacks. We can see her dad throwing the mom on the floor and swearing at her. She would hide her sister in the other room to protect her. When the foster mom tried to help her put it on, that was the last straw. *Don't touch me! I hate you!* The panic inside of her started to show and she couldn't control herself, the yelling was coming from her as she couldn't control it anymore. The foster mom didn't understand and they fought so much that both had become withdrawn. They were scared, but they didn't know how to address or even recognize the issues. The young girl, starting to feel better, walked into the room while the foster mom was on the phone with the caseworker. Having seen this so many times before, she knew what was coming: Her next removal date. Scared, she ran upstairs to her room and she cried, staring out the window. Sure enough, the caseworker's car was coming down the road. Her face crumbled with emotion as she started throwing her belongings into her worn out garbage bag once again. She went to the window to see him closing his door. It was becoming too real for her. She paused as he suddenly went to the back of the car and opened another door. Bending over, he picked up a little blonde-haired girl that looked just like her. It didn't take very long to see her reaction. Stunned. Disbelief.

Unfathomable joy. She couldn't believe this was happening. Her eyes got big and in slow motion she jumps up from the window to rush and reunite with her little sister. I love this story, and watching it felt so real. These are foster care emotions.

If you felt the emotion yourself as you read this, then maybe you can understand the complexity of these fostering emotions. They are intense and they are real. Every placement, except one, that we have ever had came as a sibling group. Twice the siblings were separated at first, and we chose to take in another sibling to keep them together. I had the opportunity, or challenge, to decide if I could handle the other sibling. It wasn't an automatic yes. Things became more trying and difficult as we brought in the siblings, but part of protecting children is doing everything you can do to keep them together. You can't expect a child to come to you and feel complete when part of them is literally missing. My mom once said that the connections we have with siblings are the strongest, because genetically, they are most like us. Even closer than with one of your parents. It is the combination of both. No one else in the world is like you and your siblings. For some reason when people consider fostering, they just picture one child. It is rare that there is only one. Be willing to take more, or at least consider it. We were scared to take in some of the kids that we had, just based on the little information that the caseworker would tell us. My life would be drastically different, and boring, if we had not decided to take Tabitha. There would have been a piece missing in our family, and the scary part is that we wouldn't even have known. We didn't have enough room, so we promised the state that we would build on to our home so that we could take her. The state didn't pay for that, we chose to do that all on our own. We used the money that we had been saving up for the garage that we had always dreamed about. Most of the time, you will not need to sacrifice too much in order to take in a child, but what if you never tried? These kids are being forced to leave their parents and their homes, and they need someone who will do everything they can for them. Is there a piece missing from your family puzzle? Can you start to feel the call? Do you have some calmness that a foster child needs to help with their chaos? I think you would be surprised if you really looked inside yourself.

Meeting Mike Jones:

Learning from an inmate about love and the human being culture

We had entered the prison as a small group of people. We had to sign in and wait until we were all present. We were escorted by the warden through the building, as he continually glanced back to get a headcount and make sure that we were all accounted for. As we entered the conference room, we could see diagrams of the prison cells and examples of weapons that had been confiscated from the inmates. One whole contained was filled solely with homemade tattoo guns made from old handheld cd players. We got to see examples of the different colors of the stripes that the inmates wore. We were seated and watched some news clips about this purgatory and the interviews that they had with the prisoners. One news program had a journalist go undercover for a day to see what it was like to be locked up. It was solemn as the warden told us that the main people in the video were no longer there, because they had ended back in jail somewhere else, or one had even overdosed. The warden left the room, locking us in, and went to go get the prisoner who would be addressing us tonight. The door opened and he walked right in. His stripes were lime green and white, which look freshly laundered against his skin that was as dark as an Oreo cookie. His large stature and strong demeanor filled the whole room. The warden grabbed a chair and put it directly in front of our two rows and he sat down. His cuffs were shiny and he had accumulated no scuffs on them yet. We didn't know how to start the conversation. Was it one of us that spoke first? Would he have anything profound to say to us? Some of the parents looked a little squeamish. Not me. Maybe it was my younger age, compared to the rest of them, or the fact that I had wanted to do this for years, but I was excited. He didn't waste a beat.

"I am in for manslaughter, having killed a person. I stabbed them 23 times and decapitated the head. I was on death row but now I am serving 1-20. My name is Mike Jones."

That was his introduction. He had no hesitation and just started telling us about his stay in the Washington County prison. A group of us foster and adoptive parents had been invited to tour the purgatory and meet an inmate. Now I don't know if it is the Criminal Minds fan in me, or the psychology background, but this was always on my bucket list, so I was really excited to finally get this experience.

We got to listen to Mike council us for about an hour and it was one of the most fascinating hours of my life. He was raised in Baltimore, about 45 minutes from our Nation's capital, Washington D.C., and he warned us that those were both extremely violent places. Even the cab drivers were so nervous about certain areas in those cities, that they would stop before they arrived at the destination and urge the rider to get out so that they weren't putting themselves in danger. Mike had grown up in the hood where the Baltimore riots occurred. His family structure was very weak and he didn't grow up with a father figure. Although he lived deep in the hood, his mother worked very hard at many jobs so that he could go to school in the suburbs which gave him educational opportunities that she dreamed of for him. Even though he was able to go to school in a safer place, the culture where he lived didn't accept the idea of him bettering himself, so they would gang up on him. He even described himself as "Urkel-esque, with a very wimpy small stature", leading him to be picked on his whole life. That was years ago, as now he was huge and obviously knew his way around a gym. He said that he does about 2,500 pushups a day to get so big, mainly to protect himself.

He spent several years in the military on both the East and West coast. He had worked hard to be where he was in life and was very successful at his job. He enjoyed working for his family and gained many great experiences. It only took one moment where he had a loss of control to change his life. He commented that he would never put blame on anyone else for his moment of rage, he felt that the military had trained him very well to escalate, but lacked the training on how to de-escalate. He had a wife and four kids with her, who now have no relationship with him since he has been in prison. He doesn't even know where they are. His oldest son is my age. He would love to be able to talk with them and loves them very much, but his ex-wife didn't reciprocate these feelings. His kids even ended up going into foster care for a short time because of his actions. Many things have changed since he has been in prison. Several presidencies had passed and he has been out of touch with much of society. He has been in prison so long that the last phone he remembers having, was a flip phone with a green screen on the front. The thought of a phone that talks back to him makes him a little suspicious, so he is reluctant to make that switch when he receives his freedom.

So why is Mike worth writing about? Because he is brilliant! Within a year of starting his sentence, he got lined up with the Hope program, which helps him set goals and progress even when he is behind bars. He has a love for reading and books. He started taking classes, and he has earned two degrees, which had to do with psychology and sociology. One foster parent asked how he learned how to communicate so well, and to which he told us that he had taken several inter-personal communication courses. After he took the courses he would turn around and start teaching them to other inmates in a classroom setting. The way that he talks was both precise and profound. He has an educated vocabulary and does not stumble upon his words. He is so clear about his life and knows completely who he is, and it is refreshing to hear him speak.

Then he talked of God. He had found God while in prison, a story that we have all heard before. He says that it was his pleading with God that allowed his sentence to be reduced to a number of years in prison instead of his original sentence of death.

Because of God, he lived. He worships with the Calvary bible study group, and even leads his own group at the prison. He won't allow other inmates to use God as an excuse. He says that it is pretty easy to spot when someone has "Found God", but you can tell from their actions they have clearly left him at the door. One of the foster parents who sat directly in front of him, was very upset because she was struggling with her daughter who has an older teenager. Her 17-year-old was dealing with depression, suicide and cutting. He stopped her mid-sentence, and adamantly attested that they get this behavior from the media. The shows on tv, YouTube videos, music they listen to and movies they go to glorify any kind of self-harm. It always existed, but now that they can see others and learn from them anywhere on the internet, they want to do it too. Mike stated that the best thing she could do was to get off of social media as fast as she can. Then he asked a doozy of a question.

"How often do you pray?"

"Probably…10 to 15 times a day."

"That's incredible. Now how often does your daughter pray?"

"…She doesn't. She stopped praying, reading her scriptures and writing in her spiritual journal about a year ago."

"Boom! That's it. She has put the social media craze before her God. Don't they know? He is EVERYTHING! I spend my day praying, because God is the one that got me off of death row. Let them turn to God, he is vast," he said as he opened his arms to the heavens looking up, "he is everywhere."

It was easy to see how this comment affected the mother and father of the young woman. I felt compelled to raise my hand and let them know that I had adopted a teenage girl who had also dealt with these self harm issues. As soon as she discovered her own relationship with God, not pushed by us, but gently guided, her self-harm had mostly stopped. I myself had never made the connection. I hoped it wasn't just that relationship with God, but maybe I had a part in helping her feel safe so the behaviors could nearly stop. If it took me and God working together to help this girl progress, then that is a great example of teamwork in my mind. This mom's eyes started to well up as she saw that maybe there was hope for her daughter, and this was a regular biological daughter too, not a child pushed through the fostering system. The allure and toxicity does not limit itself to "troubled" kids, it is free to reach anyone.

Mike then asked us if we foster kids of different ethnicities. All of us had at some point. His advice was that once we welcome them into our home and our culture, don't try to shove their culture back down their throats. We were a little confused and asked why. His response:

"We need to teach them that the connections we make with our family, even as foster families, can overpower the forces of their ethnicity."

We were silent because we didn't know what he meant at that point. Did race not matter? Were we supposed to ignore it? No. What he clarified to us was when we try to push adolescents toward their original culture, we are essentially telling them that they are not fully a part of ours. They need to know more than anything that they fit in with us and that we want them there. He has seen many young guys come into the prison system for something really low key and quite frankly, stupid. They get hooked up automatically with 'their' culture that they appear to look like, and this actually leads to the different gangs forming. He talked about the crypts and the sharks, how they are really gangs that exist in the prison culture. He rattled off about five others as well.

"Forget your culture," he says powerfully, "it is time to teach them that they are not supposed to be part of segregated races. Teach them to be part of the human race. We need to as a society, create a culture of human beings."

He doesn't want us to shove who we are to the back of the room. He wants everyone to feel loved. He probably said the word love around 50 times in this hour. He has had 18 and a half years in prison with his rights and privacy stripped from him to contemplate what really mattered. Love was his answer. When your kids have so many questions, sometimes we don't have the answers. What we do have is Love.

"We can't fill in the answers to the 'why' questions. All we can do is show love. We don't talk about love. It is an action word. Show people around you that you love them. Show them how to be a vital member of human being culture."

Another foster parent told Mike that just that day he was dealing with two of his foster son's probation officers because they had found a little bit of trouble. For the first time Mike started to show his emotions raising:

"Tell them to knock it off! Get out now and grow up before they end up in here. Let me ask you this question, do you listen to your kids?"

Everyone nodded in unison. I think foster parents, especially of teens, spend most of their mental capacity and time trying to figure these kids out.

"Yes of course." The man responded.

"Well I know you hear them but do you actually shut up your mind and LISTEN? They are telling you what they need. These are your kids. Even if you are just their parents for a short time. It doesn't matter. Right now you are their parents and they need you to listen more than anyone else. Even if you haven't grown to love them yet. No one expects you to love them right way. But what you need to do is SHOW them the love. There is an incredible difference between the two. The actual feelings of love will come in time, but the actions need to start on day one. I don't want to see your boys in here. Tell them that they have to straighten up now so they don't have to meet me. I make it one of my goals to scare the young kids so they never want to come back. I even made a young punk piss himself once because I told him if I ever saw him again that he would be violated by every man here. So far it has done the trick."

Awkward silence commenced, but his point was very clear. We knew what he meant. He saw a teenager in the second row who he thought looked bored, he called out to her.

"Hey girl back there. You bored? You don't look like you're having much fun here…..Oh you just had dental surgery? Well ouch! I might be looking that same way too, but let me tell you something. And I want everyone to talk to their teenagers this way. So just listen up. No matter what you face, you've got people that are going to be there for you. Feel good about who you are and what you're about. See, you are given a chance right now to make your own chapter in this life. Write a good chapter. Write your own story. Okay? That's how you do it," he said as he addressed the rest of us. Then he turned back towards her one last time, "And what I said was true."

If only we could all talk like Mike could. He talked about going through adversity. We are not meant to go around it. We are meant to go through it. That's how we grow. He is proud of his lime green stripes. It means he has the highest level of freedom of the prisoners. He is able to go into the community and work, so that's what he does. He is not limited to running bible study. He keeps Washington County beautiful by cleaning the highways. He keeps cars 'respectable looking' by working at the car wash. He even plants and works in the community garden. He gets to leave during the day because they know that he will come back. He always comes back, because when he leaves this place, he wants to leave it the right way. He has grown to love St. George. When he gets released in a year and a half, possibly sooner, he is going to get his house straightened up and his family back in order back in Maryland. Then he will move back here to be a part of the community from the inside. Even literally being imprisoned here, he has grown to be part of the community. He wants to use his degrees to keep others out of trouble. The sheriff even has a letter of recommendation already written for him.

He ended his time with us by reminding us about a few things. There is a molecule in our body that is different from the others. The Laminin molecule is shaped like a cross. So whenever you are feeling disconnected then we can think of that. There is a representation of Him which is inside of us. When we are going through the difficult times in our lives, we are never meant to go through the adversity by ourselves. There are always people and groups that will support us and we can connect with. Never forget to tell the natural kids that they are loved. This is difficult for them too. Tell the foster kids that they are loved. They need to find love wherever they go. They are both going through immensely tough things. Your natural kids are going to feel pushed to the side like they don't belong. Your foster kids will feel like they are on the outside and can't break the barrier to make it on the inside. Just love them. Graft them in. You can't shove them into your family. They can't live like that. Graft them in slowly so that they can assimilate to your own natural family, and in turn, to the normal world. Before his time with us was finished, I told him that the day before I started writing a book about foster care and asked if I could include his name and story. He said he would be honored to be a part of educating others.

When he was done speaking he stood up and the warden rushed to his side to escort him out. Just like that, Mike Jones was gone. He had entered into our lives for that short hour, and disappeared just as fast. When the door closed we all sat there for a minute. We wondered aloud several things:

"What had led him to a moment of pure anger that would affect the rest of his life."

"Look at how much he progressed!"

"I wonder if he will be able to track down his kids on Facebook."

"How did someone's life change so much for the better by being in jail?"

Most of all, "will he make it?"

This last one was asked to the warden when he came back from delivering Mike back to his cell. All he did was shrug, not really caring either way, and said "We'll see." And that was that.

We were then escorted back out of the prison, but as we passed a hallway, a black head popped out of one of the rooms. Mike was waving at us as we passed his door. He had a giant smile, as he yelled goodbye to us. As a foster parent, I learned so much from this little adventure. I am grateful to Mike Jones and his insight, and hope he knows that there is a little group of foster parents in Southern Utah who love him and will root for him.

Shopping Escapades of a Foster Mom

Taking kids shopping

When children come to stay at the children's shelter after being in unsafe circumstances, the first thing we do is to inventory their possessions that they have with them and fill out a personal belongings checklist. If I were to inventory my own children's belongings, I would use a notebook of lined paper, categorized into various sections. For example, one section could be doll clothes, but it doesn't really end there does it? Sure, you have your doll clothes, but are you counting the barbies? What about Monster High dolls? Did you remember the stuffed animals that have their own clothes? Do paper dolls count? How about the plastic figurines that have removable clothes? Of course, we can't forget about the beloved American Girl collection. Page one would look something like this.

1. Doll Clothes
    a. Barbies
    b. Monster High
    c. Stuffed animals
    d. Paper dolls
    e. Figurines
    f. American Girl

My point is, we are really a society that has so many possessions that it gets hard to fathom how much we really have. Here are a couple things that I do believe when it comes to most people who live in the middle class: We are pretty good at watching what we spend our money on. We work basically paycheck to paycheck. When kids go shopping with us and ask to buy fancy toys, we have our memorized list of reasons that we cannot just go out and purchase the toy that day. We like to occasionally make promises that when a gift giving holiday comes around then we will THINK about getting something similar to that. Putting food on the table and heat in the home as well as gas in the cars becomes top priority. This is a very average way to live. I also run my home like this. We look for sales, or even better, clearance sales. We go shopping with a list and clip coupons if we are ambitious. Clothes shopping doesn't happen quite as much as our kids would like it to, but they generally have clean matching clothes. Some weeks we have to eat a little less so that the kids don't have to skip a meal, but things seem to even out. I do think that this culture unfortunately has to rely on credit cards a little too much. Even that is okay though, because we are working and things are running smoothly in our homes. Even if we have a slight panic attack when we see the emergency bills for a piece of glass falling on your daughter's foot one night, or your high schooler's mandatory school band and French fees that I'm pretty sure didn't exist when I was her age….we are still the lucky ones.

I will say it time and time again. We are SO blessed and fortunate to be living in the land of the free with everything that we have. I could rattle off a hundred things that would make life a touch more comfortable. A she-shed for my sewing and crafts for example. As well as a garage for storage and keeping the cars inside during the colder months. A time share would be heavenly. Who cares though? I have exactly everything I need. I have just enough to help someone else who needs just what I have. Food. Shelter. Clothes. Love.

When it was just the two kids and I decided for sure for sure that we would start fostering, we had a spare room. It was empty and had been used as a guest room or a place for our exchange students to call home for months at a time. We had an extra seat in the car. They told us that's all that we needed to get us started. And you know what? They were right.

When I first got licensed we waited around for about 5 weeks. The room sat empty and it was calling for us to fill it. The closet was bare and we had a mattress on top of some bricks. You couldn't see the bricks, but it still wasn't the most glamorous makeup of a room. When I brought the first boy into the room he had his empty school backpack and a garbage sack full of stuff. We spent days going through it. Mostly it was a few pieces of dirty clothing that he grabbed from his messy floor in a rush. He had some empty dvd cases and half eaten granola bars. He had a Book of Mormon that the local LDS missionaries had given him. A few professional wrestling trading cards fell out of the bag. The rest of it was pretty much just junk that was lying around in his room. To the looks of it, he must have had two minutes tops to collect his things. That was it. How is a kid supposed to survive off of this?

The basics

Can you think of a few things that I did not list that should have come in the garbage bags? Reading material, toys, school supplies, family pictures are a few. Think simpler. Deodorant. That is a basic need that this kid was missing. A clean toothbrush is another. A pillow would be nice. Fortunately, in our long wait we anticipated and planned ahead for this. As he was going to bed the first night he asked "what about underwear?". My first reaction was ….*what ABOUT your underwear?* What did he mean? Is he not wearing any? Is it dirty? Was he talking about the next time he needs new clothes? Is it the wrong size? Do they have far too many holes than are actually required, or acceptable? One of these options was correct. What ABOUT underwear? This was not something that I had planned for. It was like a bombshell. As I do laundry for my other two kids I always notice how many dirty and clean pairs are thrown in there. They must rotate through several pairs a day just for fun. We find it under couches and behind beds. Stuck in between the washer and dryer. I always make sure that they have enough. But now I have a kid who doesn't. Every placement we have ever had has come to me with similar questions that just blow your mind. It leaves me humbled. And sad. And determined. I went out the next day and hit the Walmart isles to make sure that we had underwear in all sizes.

Here's the thing though. They grab what is important to them. That Book of Mormon was given especially to him. It didn't matter that it only cost a couple of dollars. He didn't care about going to church with us, in fact he resented it for the first several weeks. He loved that he owned something. The wrestling cards represented something that his ethnic community loved. I can still name more facts about John Cena than I would like.

Every kid is so different in what matters to them. One of my kids came with a can of peaches. By this point I had been fostering for several years and knew that to her it was not just a can of peaches. I always kept them in my mind and slowly pieced the puzzle pieces together over the next few months. I knew that they were important so I asked her if I could write her name on the can with a Sharpie. She said yes. I put it on the highest shelf in the pantry that I could reach and it stayed there for months. No one mentioned it, the can was just waiting. A few weeks after this I was reading the emergency shelter report of what happened that night that she was removed. Her mom had been given numerous warnings to get the house up to code. One of the warnings was to get food in the fridge and the animal feces off the ground. The house was home to dozens of transient families over the years. One of them had left the can of peaches before they had moved on their way. The day that this girl was removed, she grabbed the only food that was in the house. The peaches were the only thing that wasn't molding or stale. It was done out of defense. She felt bad that she had stolen it as it was someone else's but she was also just doing what she had to in order to take care of herself.

It was probably 5 months down the road when we were having peaches for dinner and she asked if she could eat her own. She ate the whole can that night. Seeing as how this specific can was so meaningful to saving her life, in her mind at least, I rinsed it out and put it in the fridge. We had just bought some string cheese, so I used the can as a holder for the cheese. It was her own holder. The other kids, four others at this point, all knew that they could have cheese, just not from this part of the fridge. Eventually the can disappeared, but so did her connection to it. I had been talking with her therapist about these peaches since the beginning. When the therapist heard that the can was gone, she cried during our session. She knew that this was a release and that we had entered a new stage of healing for our sweet girl. Never take the basics for granted. When you have too many options for dinner, or can't decide which outfit to wear that day, remember that you are blessed. We are some of the lucky ones.

Feeding the kids

Deciding what to have for dinner seems to add a lot of stress on parents, especially moms it seems. Usually the cooking parent will already know what the dinner plan is halfway through the day. If you don't know what you are making for dinner, then every hour adds a little more stress to your day. With your own kids you have the menu down and you know exactly what the kids will eat. Sometimes the little ones will go through different eating likes and dislikes, and we chalk it up to "it's just a phase". Sometimes it is, and sometimes kids just don't like certain foods. My son for example has never liked baked or mashed potatoes. We have tried to introduce it to him for 6 years now, and I think we are ready to admit that he just naturally doesn't like potatoes. He can do fries just fine, but can't stand the other forms of them. This is really easy to get around when making dinners. Other kids do the usual stages, hating mushrooms, onions or tomatoes. That's all normal. Feeding foster kids is very much like having a sleepover and serving them dinner. I don't know that I have ever hosted a sleepover and had every kid enjoy everything we served. We can even run into tricky spots when we are serving pepperoni pizza.

So what makes it so different? For one, you are preparing food for people that you don't know. If my son were to go to a friend's house and they served mashed potatoes, they wouldn't know that it would be a negative experience for him. I have a toddler who lives off of cheese, so they might also have a hard time feeding her as well. It's not a reason to look at the kids in an undesirable light, it is just something to be aware of. I have heard of some moms making a certain dish for their placements on the first day. Some moms do pizza, one did tater tot casserole. Most of the food questions in my life can easily be answered in one word-PIZZA. This seems like a great go to, and I have never gone wrong with this plan. It is my backup plan. The most ideal option would be to ask the kids what they would feel most comfortable with, and if it is early enough in the day then I can make it for them. We have had some kids arrive as late as 7 or 8 pm, so that doesn't always work. My adopted daughters both came on birthdays of people in our family, so we were already having really fun food (pizza, you guessed it) and cake.

Here's the thing though, there is going to be mixed reactions no matter what with these sweet foster kids. When my teenager came the first night, for instance, she didn't eat for several days. She was so upset and scared. When she did eat, it was greasy cafeteria food (according to her), which made her sick to her stomach. Add some nervousness and fear to that mixture and food was not her friend for a while. It took awhile for her to eat at the table with us, probably at least a week. We always made sure to set a place for her, and made sure that she knew dinner was being served. In fact, a few days after her arrival, I took all five kids to my parents' house, a weekend getaway that we had already planned. She still hadn't really eaten with us, so I was able to rely on my mom to get dinner going at her house. When it was time to eat, she made sure all of the kids were at the table with hands washed and ready to pray. My mom probably didn't know that we had been awkwardly tiptoeing around the food issue, so this was a nice fresh breath of air when it happened naturally. It is at these first meals when you notice what food the kids will eat and what they won't touch. Their eyes will sometimes get big as if they see random body parts in the food as they pass it to the next person.

Food is a very tricky subject for kids in foster care. Legally you can't deny them food, although you do hear of the horror stories. I'm not talking about those situations, just the normal day to day foster families. If a child doesn't want to eat your food, that is fine. I never make a big deal about it. You don't know what their bodies and minds are going through. If they pass the tuna noodle casserole, and the green beans, and the fresh fruit, and the dessert, without taking any, it is still fine. There is never a need to embarrass them or publicly note that they are not eating food. You can either try to ask them quietly if there is something wrong, or if they can think of something that they are willing to eat. You can also wait until after dinner to address it. Several things may be going on. They could be nervous or upset and the thought of food doesn't sit right with them. There could also be food aversions or allergies that they are being cautious about. It could be food they hate, this is extremely common. It could be food that brings up certain memories that could be triggering them. It may be out of defiance- they are angry to be there, therefore they don't want to eat in front of you, another common thing. They could be sick. Maybe they just aren't hungry, or have had punishments for eating in the past. The list can really go on and on.

Sometimes, especially with the girls, they have eating disorders and eating food makes them too guilty or afraid that they will be harming their bodies. We know this happens far too often, and have learned that it is good to talk about the food that you make. We have had kids before that had a past of bulimia or anorexia. It is not exceptionally rare in the middle school or high school settings. There will be certain kids who are willing to talk about it, and there are those kids who refuse to have an open dialog. There are many reasons that these eating disorders start. The root of the problem is very often that they had distorted views about their body image. They can get this all on their own, but so much of this comes from over exaggerated portrayals of what you should look like in the media. I have spent a lot of time volunteering in the middle schools, and the things that I hear from these girls are frightening. They are much more dramatic than when I went to school in the early 2000's. It also helps to hang around great people too.

    A huge difference can be made in the home. It can really help to talk about nutrition and *why* you are eating what you do. We basically give little nutrition lessons every night at the dinner table. There are so many things that they can learn about why we eat. My kids can tell you the difference between simple and complex carbohydrates as well as the different oils that we use. They learn quickly about preparing vegetables in certain ways and the benefits they have for us. We feel it is important to teach about the energy we get from certain types of food. We use funny words in our family like okra, quinoa, millet, spaghetti squash and even the elusive word: raw. If they learn that we need to have certain vitamins and minerals in our bodies to use for fuel, they will focus on eating more produce. You can certainly live off of a produce and protein-based diet without eating too much of the fattening things. We like to teach about balance and the right kind of food. Even if the girls learn about this, and proper age appropriate exercise, and the eating disorders don't simply vanish, at least you have taken the first step. I wish I had known all of this as a teenager, it would have made me see things differently when I went off into the adult world. I didn't learn most of this stuff until I already had kids of my own.

    When the kids are comfortable with eating with you, it is a great idea to involve them in the food menu planning. Don't be surprised if the foods they list are going to be generally found in the frozen foods aisle. Hot pockets, freezer waffles, frozen pizzas, burritos, ice cream, Chinese food. When you ask them what they want, it is generally going to be frozen, but it will also be some of the foods they are most comfortable with. Fast food is often on the list as well. With our family ranging from 7-10 people at any given time, eating out is not on option very often. We also like to make most things by ourselves. We can recreate almost any fast food that we have fallen in love with. We have only ever bought bread a few times in our married life, we find it way cheaper to make your own. The kids will often prefer the homemade taquitos or calzones to the frozen preserved ones anyway.

    Whatever the reason, they often have a lot of trauma with food. There is the other side of the spectrum as well, hoarding. It is not uncommon for these kids to hoard food. It can happen for several reasons. One main reason will be that they didn't have routine access to food in their homes before. Often the parents are not able to provide food daily, and the kids will get forgotten. It is also the case many times that the parents are drunk or high on drugs and can't feed the kids. Parenting is not the instinct that will automatically kick in. Several of my kids had been living in a poverty lifestyle, and grocery shopping didn't always happen. Or they would be living off of food stamps, which is a fine program if you can use it correctly. The children should not have to fend for themselves and learn how to get food at such a young age. They find themselves coming into a foster home which has a lot of food, and there is often some reaction to the abundance of food. We will find food hiding in dressers, backpacks or under their beds. It reminds me of squirrels saving up for winter. As much as we tell them that we will have food for every meal, the natural instincts for survival are much often higher. The easiest way to help them is to let them know that there are some foods that they can get anytime of day or night. We made sure that there would always be fresh grabbable fruit and vegetables in the fridge. We used to keep granola bars and fruit snacks that we bought in bulk in arms reach, but they would disappear in just a day or two. If they want to overeat at meals, let them. With our boy placements, our food bill would usually quadruple. It's ok, really. We are teaching them that they have what they need and providing them with a healthy lifestyle.

Back to school

A word of advice, prepare for back to school shopping. Get yourself ready mentally for the financial responsibility that you have for them. They love name brands. They have this intrinsic desire in them to be "the same" as their classmates. Once they hit pre-teen age, plan on having them pick out their own clothes. Before that age, you can pretty much go find clearance sales and buy the clothes year round.

For some reason shoes are a big deal. We once had finished the back to school shopping, and let the birth parents know that it was done. When they found out that we bought shoes at Payless or Walmart, they shuttered and asked us to return them. The next visit the kids were gifted shoes from their parents. Each pair was about $150! That was a shock for sure. The kids just grabbed them and wore them like they were made of gold. The thing about kids shoes, is that they really only look good for a few weeks. Then you start to see the holes and discoloring. We went back to the reasonably priced shoe store the next month and replaced them with that would work out just fine. I don't have a problem with the parents buying nice things for the kids. That is completely their right. I also don't really have a problem with them snubbing our choices. It is just a good lesson that we are from different kinds of families, and the kids will be used to different types of things. For some families, dressing in name brands clothes is a priority, so get creative and see if you can make it work in your budget.

You will most likely have to start from scratch when buying clothes. Plan on getting a lot of things that your other kids would already have. Buy everything in bulk, because they will use the supplies if you want them to feel loved, get them some special pens that they will need to take care of. Sparkly gel pens are so fun for them. They also really like their own water bottles. The cheap under-a-dollar ones melt in the dishwasher, so grab a few of each kind if you don't want to get a more durable one.

This is also a great time to make sure you have enough pairs of socks and underwear. These are things you can pick up throughout the summer a few items at a time so you don't have to add to the main school supply price. Another piece of advice, try to do your shopping alone! I like to put my kids (and husband) to bed, and shop Walmart alone with listening to music with headphones around 9 or 10 pm. The store is emptying out, and you can be in your own little world. You would be amazed at how much of a difference this makes. You can choose what relaxes you or spoils you the most. Some would benefit from low key classical music. Disney music might motivate others. I have even streamed the current show I am binge watching as I am choosing which pack of dry erase markers I would prefer. Go on a date with yourself. I have also done back to school shopping with five or six kids in tow, and you end up resenting the kids because of the cost of the supplies. They will still love the things you bring home, it's like Christmas when they get to see all the loot you have for them. You get to lovingly think of the kids as you know they are fast asleep in bed. Kids are so innocent when they sleep.

Change your attitude and change your experience- and just do everything with love. These kids may not come with much, and it will be a sacrifice for you and your family. Keep a record of what works for you, look for those clearance banners, and do all things with love. Life is so much easier that way.

Was it the best of times or the worst of times: You decide

Is there really such a thing as a bad experience in foster care? Well sure, but isn't it really all about the perspective that you have on the experiences. I think so. My husband once heard that if you pray for trials, you will get them. His thought was that if you make it through the challenges then you will be a stronger and better person for it. So we tried it, or rather, he tried it- without letting me know at the tie. That was a doozy of a month. It started with the heat going out on our house, so we were slowly freezing to death, without even noticing it. We had to figure it out by having visiting family members over for Brandon's birthday party subconsciously inform us by refusing to take off their winter snow coats when we were dining. Soon after, the pipes froze under the house, breaking them and flooding the crawl space under the house. What a nightmare. With the extra bills we were incurring with the plumbing and heating technicians, we couldn't afford any more food, so we no longer went grocery shopping. Then, all in the same month, I was parking at the college on my way to class, and the Oldsmobile cutlass supreme, our first car, suddenly started smoking and flames started coming out from under the hood. My car was on fire! We eventually towed it to the mechanic, only to have our other car, literally in front of us, also catch on fire. What are the chances? Now our cars were undrivable, we had no food, no heat, a flooded house, and had to move into my parent's basement. It was about this time that Brandon finally confessed that he knew why all of this was happening- he had prayed for trials.

Being the newlyweds that we were, I was not sure I could handle anything else. Our luxuries were all dissipating in front of us at intense speeds. Did we consider this month a bad experience for us? If you ask Brandon, I think he would say that he was just enjoying the ride, because he knew what to expect. If you asked me at the time, I would have announced I was done with the trials and just wanted everything to be magically back to normal. Yes, I would have at the time proclaimed it a bad experience. A decade later now, however, I would say that I have a totally different point of view. Instead of calling it a bad experience, I would change it to a *growing* experience.

You may be asking, what does this have to do with foster care. Using our logical brain, we can make our experiences into a mathematical equation, and it could look something like this:

challenges + (x)attitude = your reaction leading to the type of experience that you *choose* to have

What variable are you going to plug into your formula?

Challenges + (whiny) attitude = challenging whiny experience

Challenges + (horrible) attitude = challenging horrible experience

Challenges + (bitter) attitude = challenging bitter experience

Let's try to determine the outcome by looking at the formula with different types of attitudes. Add a constant to your formula (you can do that, it's your attitude we are talking about here!)

Challenges + growth + (insightful x positive attitude) = a positive, insightful, growing experience

Challenges + learning + (humility x positive attitude) = a positive humble learning experience

How does this change your perspective? Let's use an easy example to show us how this works.

Scenario 1: Using a **horrible** variable

You are at home doing the dishes and planning your shopping list when you get a call that your foster child has stolen a book from the school library. Your first reaction is likely to be alarmed or angry that the child has broken a rule and embarrassed you. Give yourself ten seconds to wallow then collect yourself. Now plug in a variable.

Challenges + (horrible) attitude = challenging horrible experience

You grab your purse and storm into your car, slamming the doors as you go. Emotions continue to escalate as **horrible** thoughts race through your mind.

How could they do this? Why would they do this to me? I am going to be so mad when I see them and give them a piece of my mind. They will regret stealing that book and breaking my trust.

If you actually gave yourself those few seconds to process and calm yourself down first, if needed at all, then what happens next is completely up to you. No one is telling you to escalate your temper. You have an adult brain and should be able to choose logically how you react.

You continue to the school and see your child in the front office sitting scared on a chair. They are already terrified because they don't know which attitude you are coming into the experience with. They have already possibly seen you approach past scenarios with positive and negative variables added to your attitude. Every second matters here. They will be hyper aware and in tune to every glare, eye roll, clenched teeth, voice change and words you choose to use. If you are exhibiting these characteristics by now, you have already done some damage to the situation. They are going to feel the anger and the conversation that follows is going to overflow into their version of the experience. If your first instinct is to raise your voice and throw out groundings, then they are going to be limited in their ability to try to explain or remedy the situation. If you have already decided that the kid has intentionally stolen the book, and are not willing to listen and have an active, productive conversation, your horrible experience will start to form. After all, that is the option that you have already chosen to create.

Even if you find out that it was an accident or a misunderstanding, the experience is already a horrible one, because of the variable that you had plugged into the equation. The effects are going to be astounding if you go into these situations pegging the child already as **horrible**. The problem with the relationship at that point becomes your doing. Children are still impressionable and learning, even the teenagers. If you have already labeled them as a certain type of child, you have already damaged any future situation.

Scenario 2: Using a growing and insightful variables

You are at home doing the dishes and creating your shopping list when you get a call from the school alerting you that your foster child has stolen a book from the library. Take the ten seconds to let it sink in, and dissolve any negative thoughts before you react. You let the school know that you will be there soon to have a talk with the child. You ponder on your way, about how to make this a teaching opportunity. You quickly scroll through the trainings you have had and try to pick out a few examples that relate to this situation. As you park at the school, you find yourself closing your eyes, taking a breath and plugging in your insight variable. Taking one extra minute will be ok if you are choosing to go into the school with a positive attitude. (When I am personally walking up to the schools when I am called in, I put on the biggest cheesiest smile possible when I know no one is looking. This is not for anyone else's benefit, just for me. Since smiling releases endorphins and serotonin, I try to purposely do it as much as I can when entering a stressful situation. I need the best me if I am going to try to teach a learning lesson.

When you walk in the door, and your child sees you, it is ok to give a little smile and wave. They are already either scared or angry, possibly confused. Choose your words carefully. They may not hear all of them. Don't jump in automatically with accusations and consequences. There are numerous many reasons they could have taken the book. Here are a few that you may not have thought of when driving over to the school.

1. They didn't want to stand in line to check it out
2. They didn't understand the checking out process
3. They thought it wasn't a big deal and no one would notice
4. They forgot or are absentminded
5. The class was leaving and they thought they would get left behind, so they panicked and took the book
6. They are curious about something personal that the book talks about, like puberty, and wanted to learn about it in a discreet way
7. They are trying to be rebellious and stole it on purpose. Honestly, these reasons would apply to biological or foster children. They are natural children's instincts.

What happens next is up to you. Make sure you listen. Talk rationally, and make it a teaching moment. Share your **insight**, and gain some of theirs. Work as a team to figure out how to fix the situation. Teach them how to **grow** and learn from this. Teach them out of love. It may not be your favorite hour of the day, but hopefully you were able to control your own reactions and have an overall positive experience instead of a negative one.

We get what we make of it. Going back to the praying for challenges story, I admit, I was scared at the time. We had just enough money to get through our daily poor college life, which we loved, but we were not equipped to handle any curveballs that could be thrown at us. Once I learned that these experiences were prayed for, I had to look at it from a spiritual perspective, and that changed everything. I decided pretty quickly to change my variable to a positive one, so that we could start enjoying our experiences.

I think that what my husband and I got out of it was more strength in our relationship so we could handle bigger trials that would come later in our marriage. We also received knowledge about basic things, such as working with handymen, and learning how our house was built and dealing with the homeowners' responsibilities. We learned that the pipes need to have heat and insulation so that they can do their job. We learned that car repairs are inevitable and we always need to have a backup plan. We learned that there are people that we need to reach out to when we are having a crisis. It is ok to give up your pride and move back in with family. When we ran out of food, we learned of the local school and community food banks which were established to help people. We can now help give back to them when we have the opportunities. We learned what we can do to have our food storage filled enough to get our family through the emergencies. We learned how to fully build our family and the resources that we need. It doesn't start out like that for young newlyweds, you have to learn together. I also used this experience to learn spiritually that we are so blessed and have so many things. It was the luxuries that gave out on us. We weren't literally stranded, it would have only taken us 8 miles to walk anywhere in town. We were able to use community resources and humbly learn how they can assist our family when truly needed. We learned about collecting cans of food and are now experts at assembling cheap meals, making our own breads, tortillas and bagels, and freezer meals. We learned household skills that we still practice, while remembering how lucky we are to even have a home. So much of these skills are attributed to that tough month. We have grown so much, and are able to look around and notice when others may be in similar circumstances so we can help.

We have had some really tough challenges that we didn't expect. With this formula that we have learned, we are able to retrospectively look back and change our attitudes into whatever we want. If we want to have a bad experience with a foster child, you can sure focus on that and that will be what you believe. One thing you can do is when you are having a really hard time with one or more of the kids in your home, think about the why and see things through their perspective. It has very little to do with who is right and wrong, but more why they are behaving a certain way, which always can lead back to the life changing lessons in life that they have already learned.

Let's take hoarding for example. We once had a child that would hoard useless things and food, it didn't matter how many servings he ate at the meal, or even if he had already been eating every hour of every day. Something inside of him was telling him that he needed food at all times. It was getting really frustrating for us, because we would find a lot of garbage in his room and in his bed. He wasn't cleaning up after the mess and it eventually started getting on the walls and in the carpet. We even had an infestation of earwigs, which was our last straw. It turned into a really big deal with us and it was really straining our relationship with him. We were out of ideas. Our response was to step back and look at it, we began to analyze it, and realizing his background, provided him with any fruit or vegetable he wanted in between meals. There was no limit on those and he knew it. This seemed like decent parenting advice on our end, but in reality, maybe he needed more. The food and the process of taking all the food he could get his hands on, was the thing that he could control in his life. So he snuck the food and ate it in his room. We had mentioned this to our caseworker who brought in extra help, or an expert on the situation. She let us see that the hoarding was just a response to the emotions that he had been feeling. Eventually, when his visits with him mom got longer and more frequent, the hoarding stopped, because he was getting what he really needed, his family. Once that need was being filled, the negative behaviors started to go away. We could easily take this and say it was a bad experience, but then we couldn't learn anything from it.

Why bother putting ourselves through the challenges if we are not going to learn and grow and progress from it? To answer the question, no, I wouldn't say that this was a bad experience, but rather an opportunity to learn some new and fascinating things about human behavior. We can still to this day refine and use these skills with our kids. I wouldn't say it was a bad experience at all, because I get to choose what kind of experience I get to have. It's all up to me.

Fake parent Part I: Kids vs. Yourself

When your foster kids don't see you as a real parent

You go into fostering with the intention that you are going to make a difference and change the life of a child. Being called mom is just a bonus, but it doesn't automatically come. How nice would that be: You bring them home the first day and get a big hug and they say 'thanks for doing this mom, it really means a lot and I appreciate it'. Yeah freakin right! Maybe if you were taking in a 40-year-old whose brain has already developed nicely with logic and wisdom, but that is not how the child's brain is wired. You are 100 times more likely to hear doors slamming and them yelling that you are a fake parent. Your first instinct is to yell back "I'm not *trying* to be your mom!!!" But wait, isn't that *exactly* what you are trying to do? Give them stable and loving parents? The words that they yell, or whisper behind your back, can really cut through you like a dagger. We never really let them see that though, not that it matters, because they aren't in the market to assess how they may have hurt your feelings. Their world revolves around themselves, and their safety. Even slamming door is their way of fortifying their safety. The darkness and heaviness that weighs down their hearts puts them right into survival mode. As they slam their door, a million thoughts race through our heads.

Thoughts from the kid's prospective:

"You are not my real mom!!!!" *Slam!*

- I am SO angry!!! I hate this place!
- Why don't they understand!!!
- I should break this picture frame. It's filled with my fake family anyways. They don't know me. I don't even know me. They don't care. They can't.
- I need to get out of here. There's the window, I should go climb out and finally escape. I could take the bus or just run until someone comes and picks me up.
- How long do I have to stay here?

- They would be better off if I just left.
- Don't they get how I feel? I've been through too much to deal with this.
- They don't really mean it when they say they care. I just want to feel loved, but I don't believe them even though they say they do love me.
- I feel so much pain. Sometimes I just want to hurt myself to let the pain release itself. Then I want to hurt myself more for being so stupid about hurting myself the first time. I feel guilty.
- They must hate me.
- I am so sad.
- I am so scared.
- I feel so alone.
- I want my mom.

From the foster parent's perspective:

"You are not my real mom!!!!" *Slam!*

- Oh no! What do I do now?
- Do I go in after her? Or wait outside the door?
- Where can I find the answer? Why isn't there a handbook?
- She really slammed that door hard. I hope she doesn't break the doorframe. I bet she is scared.
- She must feel so alone-but she doesn't want me.

- She called me a fake mom? Does she know how much that hurts? Is she *trying* to hurt me? I know I'm not her mom. Her mom is the one who put her in danger in the first place. I would never act like her mom.
- I hear a lot of noise from the room. Is she breaking things? What if she puts a hole in the wall?
- I bet she hates me.
- I am so sad- for her, that she had to go through everything in her past. I am so sad that being a foster parent is even a thing. Bad things should not be happening to children. They should be allowed to be children as long as possible.
- I am so scared- for her. What if she never opens up her heart to me. Or my family, or to anyone. I am so scared that she is going to continue to slam doors her whole life. I am scared that she won't learn to keep herself safe in the real world. I am scared that I am being a bad parent. Taking in a child is a good thing to do, right? If it is, then why are they yelling and breaking things? I am so scared that she will hurt me or my kids. I am scared about how people will judge me when she misbehaves.
- I feel so alone.
- She needs a real mom.

I would say that these internal conversations are pretty accurate in a foster care setting. Our actions and impulses can absolutely make these situations intensely worse or better depending on how we choose to react, whether intentionally or involuntarily. If you have a personality that is defensive, blunt or tends to escalate quickly, then things can intensify rapidly. Some people have a kind soft heart and are willing to sit down with you to talk to you calmly to get to the root of the problem. This may be an excellent parenting strategy, but even then, not every kid will respond well to that style. Every kid is going to be different, and so is every parenting technique. I would dare to even say that even if you were disciplining twins, you would still have to assess each situation every time. Even twins raised the same way with the same traumas would have to be addressed differently because their minds are going to react uniquely. Trauma does not show its ugly head in just a few specific behaviors. It can manifest itself dozens of ways for every child. If you are parenting the right way, you will attempt to keep track and assess these individually. It is exhausting! The nature vs nurture debate would be fascinating to study when it came to childhood trauma. The thing about fostering, is that they don't match you up based on intensely analyzed and reviewed personality tests. You won't expect to get a phone call based on your latest Myers Briggs assessment. Ideally, the caseworkers will look at the homes and try to find a compatible relationship, but there is only so much they can do when they are scurrying around trying to find any homes for the placements to sleep in that night. It takes a lot of work to be a foster parent.

What do you do when you get told you are a fake parent? Do you clasp your hands over your mouth and run to your room, throwing yourself onto the bed wailing? I would hope not. That would set a horrible example to everyone who just witnessed that behavior. Would you wait for someone to comfort you? Not going to happen, you are supposed to be the adult now. Will you have a twinge of pain in your heart? Most likely, at least the first dozen times it happens. Here's what you do. Take a deep breath. Close your eyes for half a minute and picture yourself in the eyes of your foster child. Knowing everything that you know about them, are you surprised they are acting out? It's hard to know exactly what they face when they walk around school all day. Then they come home to a home that is not really theirs. They have to open the front door that belongs to someone else. If you have biological kids, they feel that they have to keep their distance so they don't overstep their bounds. They eat food that is not cooked the same way and have bathrooms that smell differently than they are used to. They have literally been taken out of their home and placed somewhere foreign to them. It's like taking their piece off of a game board and, without their permission, putting them on a totally different square. They have no control. Of course, they are going to look at you and think "you are not my mom".

We are humans that need connections. We thrive off of connections. Even babies need touch and stimulation in order to thrive. Without it, they could develop failure to thrive. This is similar to the Harry Harlow psychology experiment that was studying maternal separation in newborn monkeys. Harlow removed the baby from its mother within six to twelve hours after being born. In one experimental group, the monkeys were placed in a cage with two kinds of surrogate mothers. Half of the mothers were made of mesh, and the other was a piece of wood covered in terry cloth, which had several soft spots on it. The baby monkeys were able to choose which surrogate it went to, as they both had the capability to feed the infant monkey. In the second experimental group, they were not awarded the opportunity to choose, it was one or the other. The group that allowed the monkeys to choose, spent most of the time cuddling with the soft terry cloth mother, even though they would get the same amount of milk as the mesh mother would provide. They were instinctively more affectionate with the terry cloth monkey. The second group that had no choice, did show some interesting results. The terry cloth monkeys grew up to exhibit normal attachment and behaviors when they were put into stressful situations. They would even cuddle with the terry cloth monkey when they felt threatened. The mesh moneys however, would instead throw themselves on the floor or rock back and forth when presented with the same stressful situations. They would not go to the mesh mother for comfort. These monkeys are an example of the innate connections that exist. Nobody wants to be alone.

Not even when a foster child slams the door. Maybe they don't want you, but they still don't want to be alone. Find ways to build the connections in their lives.

The next time they yell that you are not their real mother, then why don't you try responding this way: "Then let me be your friend." Sometimes that's all they really ever wanted. The door will open up eventually. They have to come out. This is not a Beauty and the Beast opportunity to yell "Fine! Then go ahead and STARVE!" We are nothing without kindness from others. Being a parent is not all about giving structure, rules and yelling at the little ones. Yes, they do need structure and rules, but please don't make that the only basis of your relationship. Treat them with kindness, love, dignity and respect. Notice I didn't say trust. I *wish* so deeply that I could say that you will all trust each other right away. You won't. I promise. It doesn't matter if they are two years old or eighteen years old. Trust is earned and it takes a lot of work to make it mutual. Especially with the teenagers. They have been burned way too many times and are old enough to understand the dark and scary parts of this life.

When we don't see ourselves as real parents

There will be moments of doubt when we are parenting our little kids. In our home we have had foster kids, even if it was only short term placements, from ages newborn to seventeen and a half. It seems natural to want to protect children. They are so innocent and need families. Our license plate holder reminds us that Children Need Families Too. The easiest part of fostering is deciding that you want to do it. When you feel that twinge pulling on your heartstrings, and you feel you are being drawn to the sweet children, it's easy to want to help.

Going through the foster care training was kind of a surreal experience. We learned SO much, and I love taking the classes. I went through the entire program twice, and looking back I can see why. Entering the training room is kind of like being invited into a superhero undercover meeting. Very few are allowed to enter. It's as if only the special most important people are allowed to be there. Sitting down with my husband, we were both running on adrenaline- both from nervous excitement, and also from the long car rides we had to take to get the trainings done. With our palms sweaty from anticipation, it's as if we opened the training manual to read the super-secret message for us:

Your mission, if you accept to choose it, is to take a damaged broken human being into your family. They will be a stranger to you. They may not like you. There is a chance that they are suicidal or will wind up pregnant as a teenager. They will tell you they hate you. Teachers will be frustrated with them and by proxy, you. Their parents will glare at you and swear you are their arch enemy. They may even murder you in your sleep. You will show them love and hopefully you won't screw them up even more. This message will self-destruct in three, two, one.

Needless to say, we were left with about no confidence as we finished the trainings. Some of the other people in the room are licensed veteran foster parents, who just come to renew their license or get some of their yearly training done. They tell of the most scary situations. One that my husband remembers well is hearing of a family taking two new boys into their home. They had severe anger problems and this mom was not planning on sleeping for a long time out of fear that something would happen. That night around bedtime she had heard shouting from the kitchen. She rushed in there only to be stopped in her tracks. The two boys were in the middle of an actual knife fight, pirate stance and all. The mom nearly passed out! She found the courage to make it to the next day, and every day was easier in her mind because she had already had a knife fight and hospital visit taken care of. She was able to check that off of her list of fears and move on, with experience now. Glancing over to see my husband's wide eyes as he took this story in pretty much explains how we feel coming into foster care. We are no superheroes, we are just plain crazy.

So go ahead and complement us once in a while. Every day is like another loop on the roller coaster. Every night we make it through we can high five each other and pass out on our pillows. We will always have one ear listening and one eye open as we sleep, just in case. Not out of fear, but because parenting is a 24 hour a day job. It is because we care and want to make sure they are keeping themselves and us safe.

Just because we are foster parents does not mean that we have all the confidence and experience needed. We are all just trying to do our best. Sometimes we need to flip the switch on our survival mode setting.

To the Foster parents:

You are not alone. You may feel that you are, but you are not. You have signed on for a tremendous burden. It is both the hardest and best adventure I have ever been on. You can do it. And if you can't, ask for help. Look for respite or check out some books. You have people set aside to help give you resources, find them. Let your spouse know that they are doing a great job, and let them compliment you. If needed, ask them to compliment you. Celebrate your good days, for there will be many of them. Search out other foster parents who need you. Go to lunch with them or have them over for playdates. We use bonfires to get to know people. Offer to help with their kids. Learn from their experiences and you will be amazed at how much you already know.

We are all going through similar situations. If you ever feel alone, you can always contact me. I will always be on your team.

To the friends of foster parents:

Reach out and join their village. Everyone can always use some kind words, and perhaps some chocolate. Pray for foster parents and pray for foster kids. You will never know the battle that anyone else is going through, so don't assume anything. They need to be watched out for. There is more blood, sweat and tears in parenting than anyone would have imagined. Try not to judge the kids. My life has truly been changed from knowing these special kids. I have learned to love so much more completely because of all of my kids. The world has already been against them, and they need cheerleaders. Clap for them and give them hugs because they are learning to soar. They will teach you things about yourself if you listen close enough. They have a depth greater than most children. They have already experienced heartbreak that most won't understand and they have to deal with it for their whole lives. Encourage your kids to play with them. They have had so much rejection that they need to balance it out with that much acceptance. Listen more than you talk.

To foster kids:

You are loved, even if you can't feel it. You are important and make a difference in our lives. You have a great worth and we just want to help you to see that. We may seem to range anywhere from strict to spineless. We are new to this specific day too. There may be too many rules to follow and we will expect you to work hard. We know that school is hard, and that people don't treat you nicely. We DO see how broken you feel. We also see you more clearly than you can see yourself. Trust in us. We are trying to help you become the best you that you can be. We are not trying to clone mini versions of ourselves. We know that we are not the perfect parents, but we are trying. Our hearts are full of love that we are trying to give you. Open your own heart just a crack so you can receive some of it, any of it. Every once in a while, we are going to be exhausted. Just bear with us. Talk to us, because we are ready and waiting. You are our child, and we are doing our best to become real parents to you.

We have an appliance repair neighbor who was working on our washing machine one day, and I asked him his thoughts about adopting. They had ten kids of their own, and a few years ago they adopted two of their nieces. Howard gave a nice insight. As a dad, it was actually easier to connect to the kids in some ways. Biologically, moms have a unique connection with their own natural children, so it makes it hard to imitate that bond with other kids. Women tend to naturally be nurturers because that is how we have kept our children alive. It can be harder for moms to bond with the kids because they can sense the difference. The moms have been there as the baby is growing, and they nurse the babies. When you nurse, there are actually hormones released that create a literal bond that benefits the both of you. His thought was that although they are great nurturers, women are often more complicated in the emotions and feelings departments. I don't disagree. Throughout history, he continued, dads have naturally come into the "adoptive" mindset more than we realize. Consider a deadbeat dad that has left the family. It is common that at some point, the mom will find a new partner and thus, creating a new "dad" model for the kids. Men often step in easier to help raise and rear the children that may not be theirs.

Consider single parenting for a minute. We are so used to seeing mothers raise families on their own. Society is used to seeing this happen. We acknowledge that it is hard, then move on. However, when you see a single dad, society will stop to marvel and ask how he can accomplish such a feat. Why is there a difference? When both parents are full time parents, as any parent who is present should be considered, and they work to support the family, then why do we single out and praise the fathers? I honestly believe that children benefit from being raised, or even mentored by both male and female role models in their lives. Don't confuse this with me trying to take a political stance on human rights and gender equality. I only mean to imply that characteristics from both mothers and fathers (or family members, neighbors, friends, teachers etc.) help add unique experiences to help them grow.

His thought about why it is easier for dads to connect, is because they are at a father's distance to the kids. He says having a father in a kid's life is so powerful and can be the key to raising well rounded kids. Parenting is much harder when you have to do it by yourself, partnerships are built in when you are raising kids together. Fathers have a very special part in the child's lives. They are often there to support the family financially, and help the family bond during quality family time. Brandon works very hard to keep our family in a stable situation. When he comes home for the night or the weekend, he will devote his time to the family. He catches up and helps plan our outings. The mom distance to the children is often closer, because of the way we build our relationships with our family. Whether moms will stay home with the children, work full time, or a combination of the two (that's me), they focus on being the mom of the relationship. So perhaps there is a little difference. I'm sure this could cause a great debate with people throwing their research at me, or political, or religious views. But I'm not here to debate, just to give my own thoughts.

I AM a real parent. There is nothing fake about me. I have real kids in my home. I may be your temporary parent, but I am not fake or pretend. I am as real as you are. Regardless if this is temporary, or forever, you are my real child. I will protect you and love you. I am a real parent.

Fake Parent Part II:
When society sees you as a fake parent

Have you noticed that there is a bias towards new parents? It seems as if you don't really even get credit for being a parent until you have at least three little tykes running around your legs when you are trying to have a normal conversation. Not until you can juggle school schedules, doctor appointments, play dates and food allergies- and then you are a parent. Why is this? A parent is a parent no matter how many days you have been doing it. It doesn't matter if you have twenty kids or just one. You still give all of your time and energy toward raising children. Once you become a parent, you are always a parent. Even if your children have been removed, or are no longer living. Even if you are estranged and haven't seen them, you are still a parent. Not everyone gets the privilege of being raised with both parents. I was one of the lucky ones- I got both parents my entire lifetime so far. They are married and are still in a functioning married relationship. I can't say the same for others in my life. My husband lost his mother the month before we met. His father had left the family and disowned them just a few years before. With my adopted girls, they both know their mother, but neither really knows their father. I'm not even sure if both of the fathers know about their kids. Let's give credit to the parents that are actively trying to be parents. That is how you earn the title of mother and father.

Being a new mom is hard! I remember it so clearly and am grateful that I am past that stage in life. I recall being tired all the time and feeling lucky if I was able to shower that day. I had a handle on things though. I made sure that the babies were fed, which seemed to take most of the day. They had their diapers changed when needed and they were cuddled for much of the day. They had their baths and were swaddled in blankets. I was doing everything right, because the baby was happy, loved and had their needs taken care of. There is still this strange phenomenon though, that people who have had kids before you did, must interject with their opinion. I had a family member once tell me that I needed to return a certain brand of diapers that I had been given at a baby shower. I was shocked. It was a gift given out of love to help support me as a new mom. There was no way I was going to reject a gift like that. I kept the diapers, and used every brand that I was given. This also taught me that people were not going to hold back their opinions. I also learned that I need to be cautious when giving advice. Even if I had a graduate degree in child development, there are times when opinions and appreciated and other times when you should just keep them to yourselves. Now this is not meant to offend anyone at all. Just to opposite, I just want to send the message out to the word that your words do matter and we need to be aware of how we speak to others, especially new moms. Whether or not you have had a baby, remember these few things. The mom is raw! Emotions and body. Every new mom is going to react to things differently. Having a baby is like running a marathon, you are just beat up and exhausted, even if you did manage to get some sleep and a shower.

Some things that never need to be commented on include:

1) Any reactions to the baby name they chose other than excitement are unacceptable. Names are personal and they have had almost a year to pick out the perfect name.

2) How tired they look or grumpy they act. I promise you, your comment will only make it worse.

3) Asking about having other children. This can be very sensitive for a lot of people. You don't know the journey that they have been on so don't make assumptions.

4) Anything facetious about prenatal or postpartum depression. These are not jokes and can have serious consequences. Depression is a silent and deadly assailant. You often can't tell that moms are suffering from this. Take it seriously if they do confide in you they are dealing with it.

5) Asking about having certain gendered babies. If they have already had four girls and just announced they will be having a fifth-don't ask if they wanted a boy. They literally have been thinking about baby boys since the moment they found out they are pregnant.

 Just be kind and let them know you are happy for them. Do you know many foster families? Have you ever thought about the things that are appropriate to ask them? You need to be just as sensitive when talking to us. We are also emotional and often feel like we are being run over by a monster truck. When you have your own baby, I likened it to a marathon. When running, you are experiencing everything yourself. You are in control of what you eat and when you sleep. You know when the baby is generally going to come. It wears your body out. With fostering it's a little different. This isn't your baby or child that you are raising. You didn't have control of them since before they were born. You don't always know what they were exposed to prenatally. They could have had drugs in their system, or maybe they had been neglected as babies. These can leave a lifetime of scars on their body and brains. We didn't choose the traumas that we now get to parent. Sometimes you get run over emotionally and mentally. We were not there from the beginning to help guide them when they are dealing with hard situations.

They have learned to react and express themselves in ways we don't always approve of. We did choose to start fostering, but there is so much unknown out there. The point is, don't judge others for what they are going through. We do the best with our kids whether they are biological, foster, step or adopted kids.

Even in the fostering community, I believe there is some judgement towards "new parents". Families who have never been able to have their own kids, and suddenly find themselves with new foster placements, are often seen as newbies and don't get the respect they deserve. Every minute of their days now will be devoted to trying to cope with new family members and their corresponding behaviors. These new families could use plenty of constructive courtesy. Not criticism, they can get that on their own. Go out of your way to compliment and ask how they are doing. If they have a personality similar to mine, they will just say they are doing fine and change the subject. Let them talk if they need to. Let them cry if it happens. It is not a very big support system that we are a part of. In my city, there are 35 foster families, and I don't know all of them. I see glimpses of them at trainings, but most seem to stay to themselves. Most of the people on our team are professionals, which is good and bad. If the team members are always rushed and don't take the time to focus on your family's concerns, you will get brushed out of the way. They are ALWAYS putting out fires with the caseloads that they have. They do care though, their job is incredibly taxing, and they don't usually get the credit that they deserve. It takes special people to go into social work.

In the foster care world, the biological parents of your foster kids are often not in the best shape to raise children. When the main reason for children entering foster care is due to substance abuse, physical abuse and neglect, the parenting skills are often absent. I have almost always approached the biological parent relationship cautiously and kept them at arm's length.

There are so many reasons behind this. Emotional safety comes to mind as a big one. Every person involved can get burned if they are not careful. One thing that I do not regret at all was making the decision to treat them with respect anytime I saw them. I am so glad I did. I still run into former foster kids and their parents. I'm thankful that I had the insight and instinct to always smile and say hi. You will often not need to do more than that. Sometimes it catches them off-guard, especially if they have been bad mouthing you for years to anyone they can get to listen. Other times it can be dangerous to get too close. I have had a biological mom try to stall us at the elementary school long enough for a truck to show up with family members that terrified my kids. They gave the girl presents and hugs. She was too young to know that these people were not safe in her life. They took her behind the truck and tried to talk to her without me hearing them. We had been approached several times at our car by multiple dangerous family and friends. We eventually started parking far away from the visits and walking. We even sold our cars and bought new ones. Part of the reason was to upgrade to take in more kids, but also because scary people have seen us in the car and knew our license plate. Don't let this scare you off though, because there are ways to get around this. Technically, if you don't ever want the family to see you drive up, the caseworker can be the in-between person and stagger your arrivals. They want you to feel safe too.

What does it look like to show respect to those bio parents? The easiest way it is to acknowledge when they make progress in the family team meetings. These meetings are usually held every three months or so. They will go over the progress that the parents are making because, in theory, everyone wants them to move forward in the process. Some examples of progress may be scheduling and attending therapy, even if it is just one time. Maybe they were instructed to leave a diseased relationship that was toxic to have children around. Success can be as small as getting out of bed and being dressed for the day. In one meeting I attended they told the dad to just get out of the house and make some good friends. Applaud their success and smile with them. In their eyes you are either with them or against them. You are not on their team necessarily, but the child's team. A good parent will want what is best for the child, but it takes a lot of growth to get to that point. Now that I have had a case that turned to adoption, I am in charge of the visitation with the bio mom. Having the respectful relationship during the fostering days was very important because it allowed me to set the tone for how I want the visits to go. We do go visit every couple of months, as much as my daughter asks for the visits. The mom will often bring friends and family members, because they don't want the family connection to be gone. I don't mind as long as they are being safe and appropriate. Again, I park where they can't follow me to the car.

Progress for the biological parents doesn't have to end after the kids have been officially removed and placed into an adoptive home. No one would want that. The whole point of creating placements in foster homes is to give them a safe environment to grow up in, so that they can live life as normally as possible. I had the bio mom of my kids look me in the eye every time she saw me and tell me that she is grateful to me for being willing to take both of her girls, and that she is going to continue to get therapy and make her life good again. Since the adoption I haven't brought up her therapy visits. I don't ask because the only requirement that I really need from her is to keep the relationship with our family appropriate. I expect good language, no gossip, and no empty promises. For me, that shows progress on her end. She can still be a good parent because I can see her trying to follow these rules. Way to go mom!

Not everyone sees foster parents as real parents, unless you have your own biological kids-then you know what's up. I would say that most of the parents I know who do foster care already have biological children. I know that there are many families who weren't able to have children, of their own. Then they turn to foster care, which is great as long as you know what you are getting into. Parenting starts the second you get a kid, no matter how that child comes into your life. The same is true of step families. You are suddenly a parent and have a great responsibility. Not everyone sees you as a grounded parent however. There are so many instances where foster or step parents are just treated like less of a parent, even though they may be the ones day in and day out shouldering the parental responsibilities. I have heard of step parents not being allowed into the emergency room when bringing their child in. If they are raising the children, so even co-raising the children with the other parents, they deserve the opportunity to admit the kid into the hospital. I see it when I walk in with a foster child to introduce myself to their teacher at school. As soon as I say foster parent their eyes often roll back in their heads in slow motion as if to say 'not this again'. This is not always the case, but it happens enough to notice. I have even had the school go ahead and conduct behavior plan meetings for the students without even letting me know about them. I want to know! I have to deal with the behavior all the time, and you need my input. It affects me in every way. I get the impression that they often see us as a temporary fix, like a band aid, and they are the surgery that is planning on fixing the child. This is not how it works. Intervention needs to come from a team of professionals working together-and guess what? I am a professional parent. Don't shun me. Don't ignore me when I insert my opinion. Don't look at me like I am *just* a foster parent. I am their biggest fan, and will walk with them every step of the way.

    I do have to mention that not all foster parents are created equal. I have only worked with regular foster parents, but I too have heard the horror stories that you probably thought I would be addressing in this book. I know there are abusive parents, or some that neglect certain children. Just as these aren't the norm in day to day parenting, it also isn't something that I would see in real life in the fostering community, but I do understand that it happens. There is a screening process, but as you know, you can't typically just look at someone and know all of their evil intentions. The obvious ones are vetted out, but every once in a while, there may be bad foster parents. I mostly see it in the movies or on the news. Maybe it is an easy story line, but I don't know why they feel the need to portray fostering in a negative light. If anything, these kids need more positivity in their lives. This is why I am an advocate for fostering. I really believe anyone who has a little room in the homes and their hearts can foster.

Sometimes you don't get enough support from your own family for fostering. I am not referring to my personal experience in any way, as my family has been great with my placements. I see it all the time though. I have friends who choose to go to family reunions because they know that the other family members will get annoyed with the behaviors or the new kids. I have seen biological children treated differently than foster children, which is hard to deal with. Christmas and birthdays can be hard, because the kids are not always gifted the same way as their foster siblings. A lot of the time, foster kids don't even receive anything from grandparents or cousins. Even if they are only in your home for a short time, it is still their Christmas too. I have heard of family members only inviting the biological kids over for sleepovers. It makes sense logically, but the foster kids are still going to feel left out. It may be best to just put events like these on hold, so as not to exclude anyone. Make a note of the kid's birthdays and at least send a text or a card. Let them know they are being thought of that day. And foster parents, it is totally ok to text your family and remind them that it is a foster kid's birthday that day, and ask them to send a note. I've done it, and it goes over well.

There is a rule, at least where I live, that you can't post pictures or names of your foster kids on social media. We've been fostering regularly for several years, and have Facebook accounts. We love posting pictures of our family. The big struggle is that you purpose have to block certain people from being part of your story. A day at the lake looks really fun, but you can only post half of the picture, to hide one of the kids. Or you can't show your birthday dinner because there are foster kids at the party with you. It feels very much like you are hiding part of your love and being deceitful. Sometimes I think people forget that I even have foster children, because there is no whiff of it through my profiles. I feel like I have to hide the kids sometimes. The funniest thing about privacy is that foster care organizations typically have floats at parades. They ask for volunteers to ride on the floats to show off how great of a program it is-but the catch is that you can't have any foster kids on it. I'm not going to send my biological kids up there and alienate my foster kids to promote foster care. It doesn't make sense. I know it's a privacy issue, but still, these kids need me to show them off. They deserve it. I have combatted this by describing happy thoughts so that my friends and family can picture it too. That is about the time when I started blogging in my posts about my experiences. I couldn't show you, but I could tell you about my wonderful family. I have been places where people who I haven't seen in years, even decades, tell me how much they enjoy my posts about fostering. Maybe that is the reason that I am writing this book, to let you picture it all in your heads as I tell you about my experiences. Just as we are real parents, they are also real kids.

Let's put down our judging binoculars. Treat everyone with kindness and respect. Eventually these kids will all be grown up and the experiences that they go through while they are developing will shape who they become later in life. Now that I have kids finally growing up, I realize just how quickly the parenting years are zipping by. They creep so slowly at first. You hold your little baby and think, just 18 more years..and then another baby comes into the picture and you are starting the countdown over again. Suddenly we found ourselves at the opposite spectrum. I only have six years to get you to adulthood, which quickly turned into four years. We have lots to do and to teach these kids everything they need to know before they enter the adult world. I get it now when they say to cherish every moment because the times is going by too fast. It seems like an eternity for the kids, but they are growing up every second. Every second counts, and they have been right next to them. I'm not a nobody, I'm a mom.

Where's my village?

You know how the phrase goes: **It takes a village to raise a child**. Think about your current parenting status. If you are like me, I am a mom and have children that I get to raise. Are you like me? Or do you fall into a different category? You could be a dad raising kids. You could be a grandparent, a teenager, single, childless, empty-nesters. Whatever you define yourself as, this chapter is for you. I really want to impress the concept upon you that you can make a difference in foster care. All you have to do is open up your eyes and be aware. Fostering is SO exciting when you are newly licensed and ready to start taking in those kids. It's very comparable to waiting for your newborn to arrive when you are pregnant with your own baby. Will it be a boy? A girl? Twins? Quadruplets? Will they have disabilities? Will they look like me? No matter what, you are ready with both feet firmly planted on the ground, arms open and waiting for the child to arrive.

Now I've become a mom both ways. I had a baby girl, then a baby boy. After he was about 2 years old, I brought the idea of foster care again to my husband. We had considered it when we were in our early 20's and almost had finished the process when we decided we weren't ready yet. The licensing part overwhelmed us. Then we waited. SMART MOVE! I was about 28 years old when we went around the second time. I had already had the mom skills kick in and life was going very smoothly for me. It was easy and I enjoyed watching my children grow up. We got our first placements when my son was two. I'll tell you what, I had imagined my life to continue to be smooth sailing like before. I had never imagined that this year would become the most tumultuous of all. About three months after we got our first placement, I found out I was pregnant. Another two weeks after that point we had another placement. This new boy was the brother of the one that we already had in care. They didn't put both with us originally because they thought that they would be too violent and get into trouble if they were together. You know what? They were right, and it was HARD!

The pregnancy turned out to be my hardest one yet, and I ended up needing iv's and special medicine every day because I suffered from hyperemesis gravidarum and had a whole list of things that were threatening the pregnancy. I had fibroids, cysts, an anterior placenta, and was physically, emotionally and mentally drained. I could go on for hours about how hard it was, but all that matters is that in the end, I was able to have my baby girl. We kept her gender a surprise for us because we wanted something to keep us going. We were thrilled! She was unique from the first moment, the only toe head in the family with bright blue eyes. Finding any semblance of her Mexican heritage became a fun game for us.

Let's dive into an average day with these boys, with the knowledge that I didn't tell anyone I was pregnant for several months into this process. No one knew how sick and in pain I was, which ended up putting more stress onto me than necessary. Here is a typical schedule:

- 7:00 Am Wake the boys up and get them into the showers
- 7:10 AM Get the boys back out of bed and get them into the showers
- 7:12 AM *Seriously.* Wake the boys up!
- 7:20 AM They get into the showers
- 7:40 AM Start knocking on the doors so they get out
- 8:00 AM remind them to pick up their clothes off the floor and tell them that breakfast is ready
- 8:15 AM Do a backpack check. Remind them to turn in the homework that I already put into their backpacks. Give a 20-minute warning that we are leaving for school.
- 8:17 AM Do a room check. It is even messier than before. Have them individually. No separately. No individually. Ah who cares, just come help me clean this room again!
- 8:20 AM I found a library book under the bed; the same one I had put in the backpack last night. 15-minute warning!
- Check the clothes that they chose to wear. Encourage them to put on something cleaner. Change the baby's diaper.

- Pick up the broken *(insert the piece of furniture or dishware here)* that they just destroyed.
- 8:30 AM 5-minute warning. Clean up the blood and find the food they stashed under the bed. There are earwigs now.
- 8:45 AM We are now TEN minutes late, one can't find his backpack and the other is hiding. We finally leave for the school on the other side of town.
- 9:00 AM I sign the kids in because we are late while holding my daughter's hand, carrying the baby and telling the boys to stop kicking each other- or even worse, the teachers, as they walk by. I walk the younger one to class because his teacher requires me to come into the school morning and afternoon to give me reports of how awful he is.
- 9:10 AM Morning sickness hits. I have to throw up. Go back into the school while still holding my two kids.
- 10:00-3:30 PM I wait near my phone because the principal, teacher and/or behavior specialist is scolding me to come get the younger one. He has broken the *(insert expensive machine equipment here)*. He gets sent home daily. The staff glare at me and tell me that he was never as triggered as much as when he was placed with us.
- I go pick up the one kid. The behavior plan states that I must bring him home, put him in a time out in him room for 30 minutes. Then I must bring him back where they will glare at me and sigh audibly. Then I wait until they call again, usually about 20 minutes later and request that I take him home again for the same result. Then I bring him back to the school and wait until school is over so I can pick them up together. If the younger boy is kicked out again he is not allowed to return that day. We start over again the next day. I am trying to also squeeze in getting my daughter to her preschool class on the opposite

side of town as this school. I am also running a catering business and have had to turn off the oven with food in it to go follow the schools commands. Multiple food orders have been ruined.

- 3:30- 6:00 PM I pick up the kids. I'm exhausted and discouraged. And in a hurry so I can go get there before the preschool is released. I also have music students coming to the house that I need to beat home. We cry over homework and not enough snacks in the house since they snuck them last night after bedtime. Both boys are so behind in school that I have to spend about on hour doing their 1st and 3rd grade homework with them. They throw everything on the table out of frustration. Oh yeah, and have to get dinner ready and somehow deliver the food order. I haven't eaten yet today and almost pass out. The two-year-old missed his nap again and is screaming. We try to make sure they have plenty of outdoor and fresh air time. They ask for friends to come over, but no one ever does, because they get hurt or scared the first time they come. I may or may not have still needed to go to work to get my reports done, do my church assignments, hit up the PTA meeting, cook, clean, laundry, doctor's appointment, staff meetings, and still try to make having a family visit with the kids' mom super fun and non-emotional for all involved.
- Bedtime. There are kids everywhere. Chaos. The room smells. The house smells like boys. The bathroom needs to be scrubbed nightly by the boys because we have to use half a roll of paper towels just to clean up the amount of urine they have left on the floor and walls. They also have to scrub the inside because the feces is plastered everywhere. Nightly. We review the spelling/math facts from a few hours before but they stare at us with black faces because they apparently have no clue what language you are speaking.

They go to bed an hour after their bedtime. One is ripping pages out of books. Another is chugging chocolate syrup in the bathroom. They both get grounded. Again.

- Midnight. All the kids are sleeping. I can't sleep because once again, I'm pregnant. I can cry though. Usually I don't, but every once in a while, I do.

Where is my village?

My first year was pretty close to this every day. Except Saturdays where I had all four kids and tried to handle the indoor football games with as few wrestling matches as possible. There were Sundays, our "day of rest". The problem was my husband had to work every other weekend, so I had to tackle three long hours of church by myself. I even had to leave the kids alone in a very quiet and reverent meeting while I played the prelude, postlude and Sacrament meeting songs every week at the organ. I could see them running and jumping through the chapel. I could hear them crying and yelling. It was a relief the times that my husband was there, but it was so hard when I was alone. After a few months some teenagers who sat near our family started watching over the kids while I was not able to be near them. Amanda and Cari were their names. They added to my village. I didn't even have to ask, it was wonderful. They have remained part of my village, for the remainder of my placements, and eventually befriended my later adopted teenager.

As hard as this all sounds, I was always looking for ways to make sure that the positive outweighs the negative. If you look for miracles, you tend to find them. If you look for angels, they are around you, often in the form of a kind person.

I had several people watching out for me. Most of them are from my own church, which was great because those same people were also my neighbors and the people that I saw the most.

Even the smallest of things can tip the scale. You would be surprised at how one little thing can really make the difference in your outlook of your day. About a week after I got the first boy, my next-door neighbor who I didn't know very well, but had talked to several times, had knocked on the door. She had a garbage bag full of children's books that she had kept from when her two boys were little. These books held a great sentimental meaning for her. I knew that she had been holding onto the for when her boys were grown and had kids of their own. Something inside her was inspired to look beyond her sentiments and she saw someone who could use the books more. I will always remember that day. She was to become a major part of my village in the coming years. When I eventually adopted several years later, Kim and her husband Rory and their sons, Josh and Jaden, were right there celebrating with us. They were never able to have their own daughters, so they loved to borrow ours. This act of kindness impacted me so much that I decided to build a library outside my house so that other kids could enjoy books too. We made it in the shape of a house with a book shaped roof. Neighborhood kids still bring their used books for the Storybook Swap, and leave with some new books for all ages. Sometimes they even plan it for days before the swap occurs. This family even invited us over for the Superbowl when I mentioned that my foster son liked the Broncos. We had a great time. Years later, when I can't find my kids at church, they are usually with Rory or the boys. The kids love him, and not only because he always has a stash of candy just for them.

Another village member were the Sunday school teachers, youth leaders and primary teachers who taught the boys. They were tough and could handle them. If they ever weren't able to be there, then I would be called to step in and teach the class. I always went down to eavesdrop in the kids' classes to make sure that I could intervene before the teachers had to officially wander the halls, peaking into the adult classrooms until they could find me. No matter how rowdy or loud they got, they always found ways to report that it was going well.

"I just love his enthusiasm for…sports."

"He is getting better at reading every week. He will be catching up to the others in no time at all. I wouldn't worry about him at all."

"He had a lot less temper flare-ups today."

"I see that he is dramatically working on his wrestling skills. Good for him."

"There were less tears today, that was good."

    Their kind words help lessen my load every time they are spoken. I can see in their eyes that they see what the kids are going through and what we are having to tackle every day. Sometimes they mention how they wish that they could do the same. I always tell them the same thing, you are helping me more than you know. You are helping them in your own important way. I don't think I did a very good job showing my appreciation.

    Community members can also be part of my village. I took two foster kids to a Pow Wow one time because I was trying to teach them about their own culture. This was early in the beginning. I had my two young children, two foster kids and two temporary foster kids that I just had for the weekend. Naturally it was a weekend that my husband had to work. I decided to try and take them on an adventure. With six kids all under the age of 9, I'm sure I looked strange. We eventually needed to sit the kids down and get ready for the drum circle and dancers. One of the drummers was watching me cautiously, perhaps even suspiciously. What was that white girl doing with so many kids, and why were some of them clearly Native American? He kept trying to make eye contact with the darker skinned boys. He came over without acknowledging me and took one of the kids over to his drum. He gave him a drumming lesson and at the end of the day he even got to keep the drumstick. This little thing made a world of difference in the kid. I never really was accepted as a helper, more of a nuisance to the Native American community. Regardless, that man became a part of my village that day.

    I met a new friend who was a new foster mom and lacked a support base. I heard her call: "Hello, is anyone out there? *Where is my village!?*" Of course, this wasn't literal, but the theory still stands. She had posted in one of the local fostering community groups that she was going to go to the Canyon East park at a certain time and day and was hoping a group of people might come and join her. I was available that day and that is the day I met my good friend. I was in between placements. In fact, I had just said farewell to my first foster daughter that had stayed with us for the summer. She was a pure energetic ball of energy, so I was enjoying my quiet time, even though I missed her greatly. I was intending on taking a break and focusing on my new baby who was less than a year old. Even though I didn't have any foster kids at the moment, I was still a foster mom. I decided to venture out of my comfort zone and meet this mom at the park, and we watched her rowdy three Native American foster kids run around the park. They were a hyper bunch of loving kids, yet they were so sweet. This was her first placement, and I had been fostering about a year and a half at this point. No other moms and kids ended up coming, but that was alright we talked about fostering experiences and advice for at least a good hour. For the first time in a long time, I was able to finally step back and observe the loving chaotic playfulness of another foster family. The kids were very young, but old enough to run around and channel their inner Tasmanian devils. It was easy to see that we were going to be able to be an anchor for each other.

She had mentioned in that conversation that she was very nervous because she was going on a week-long trip to Disneyland with her biological son and didn't know what to do about these kids. At this point bringing them on the trip just wasn't a good idea with the amount of effort, money and getting the judge to agree to it. Plus, she was mentally exhausted and needed that break to give herself some respite. I mentioned that I loved doing respite, and the next month I did take them for about 8 days. Talk about non-stop energy! By the end of the week we had to clean off crayon from our freshly painted walls, and pack up the 26th load of laundry, scrub the floors and even the ceiling. It was a challenge, especially with my own three young children. I didn't even have a car with enough seats to drive the kids in, so I was stuck at home. I did attempt to bring them to the craft store once while my older daughter was in school. Big mistake. Apparently, their favorite pastime in stores is making eye contact, giving an evil laugh then running away while screaming at the top of their vocal range, then disappearing. I ended up buying the one thing I needed to make a wedding cake for a client and booked it out of there. It was a lot of work, and I'm not sure that I slept at all, and it was a very stressful week. It was all worth it though, when I opened the door to see my friend and her husband relaxed from the warm California Disney sun, smiling and ready to give the kids giant hugs and take them home. You could see that years of stress had melted away. She knew exactly what this week was going to be like for me. So did I. Yet, we agreed anyway.

To this day, I am so grateful that I was able to do this respite time for her. I was thankful for the opportunity that I could reach out and purposefully do something hard for someone else. I grew quickly to love those little kids. One of them even shared my birthday, and I still remember snuggling with them and reading them stories. We even had a little tushy dance we did with them when it was time for diaper changes. I purposefully forget the hard parts, because they are just little kids. They are innocent and the trials they have been through are not their faults. The kids need someone to love them, and even if it was for a little over a week, I got to be that someone. The kids ended up returning home just two months later. I saw them around town for several years and they would come up to me and give me hugs. This continued until one day they stopped, because they didn't remember who I was anymore. And that was okay. I had been a part of their own individual villages and loved the opportunity to help keep them safe.

    I am also glad I was a part of my friends' village. If she hadn't made the point to ask for some foster mom friends, I would have never had so many experiences over the years with this family and their kids. Almost a year to the date later, I did another respite for them, also three challenging kids. They ended up becoming close to our family and were later adopted by my friend's family just months before my own adoption. I have learned that I can go out of my way to build up village support for foster families around me, hoping, I suppose, that Karma would pay me back. This is a lesson for you to learn to. Look for opportunities to help and you will be blessed as well.

    The numbers of families who are fostering in my community are small enough that it's not a very big group of people who understand what you are going through. We do have monthly trainings, but you only go to certain ones, to help you reach your hours for the year. There is a campout, but one year it was so small that it was my family and one other family by the second of three days. There is a Christmas party for the foster kids, so you can meet some new people if you come out of your comfort zone. Other than that, you are pretty much on your own. We had to learn to create our own villages. We built a park and bonfire fit in our yard, and made it a point to invite plenty of foster families around the fire to bond. This became more common after we had started fostering and doing respite for teenagers. We also threw Halloween, back to school and even some dance parties. I purposely made a point to create a village for the other foster families.

I found a village at the schools that my kids attended. I have a deep gratitude for several teachers who stepped out to support me and my child. I wanted to mention a few. The principal at one of the schools, Mr. Jenkins was always being bombarded with running hugs from my Emma. It didn't occur to her that maybe he was busy, or didn't want hugs. He could see how special she was and always took a few seconds to give her individual attention. His enthusiasm is unparalleled, and he will do the funniest things for his students. He is the first one to get into the dunk tank and every year the students get to smash food onto him while he is wearing his suit and tie. He does it all with a smile and has made a huge difference in our family. The receptionist that worked with us the first few years of fostering, Mrs. Melody, always made sure to smile at Emma as she waltzed into the office. She even gave her polished rocks from her husband's rock collection. Her teacher Mrs. Clark treats her like her own child, and has seen the trials she has been through since the beginning. She had been watching over Emma since she was a baby and had known about her many visits to the emergency room as an infant. She will be known as one of the biggest cheerleaders in her life. Her therapist, Maria, is a constant in her life, and helps her work out her problems in new ways. She is also on my team and I love our talking sessions when we can really get to the root of some of the issues. She has given us both skills to use to get through the rough times. There are so many people at the school that have been there for Emma, including the custodian, special needs teachers, reading aids, and so many others. I can't thank you all enough to have shown us the patience and reason why you do your jobs, because you love the children.

I have had a small village at the middle school that Tabitha was in also. The principal was always in her corner, even though she couldn't see it. Her advisor Mrs. Brown even came to our adoption party and team meetings. Both of these ladies had also adopted as well. She had a few teachers who believed in her, like Mrs. Smith, and the band teachers Mr. Lee and Mr. Palmer. Every one of these people have touched her to her core, and were able to reinforce the idea that she is important and has a great individual worth. They would say the things that I would tell her, but she couldn't hear them from me. Every one of these people I believe would lose sleep over how to help her through her trials. By being a part of her village, they were also part of mine and I am truly grateful. Another special person in Tabitha's life is Danielle, her youth leader and friend. She brought her candy on her birthday, and write special letters and gave her pictures of Christ. She is quick to include her among her daughters and in her home.

The CASAs (court appointed special advocates) were also life changing for the girls. The ones assigned to our older girls were name Barbara and Rita. They treated these children like they were their own. They got to go to the lake, to museums, Shakespeare plays, and restaurants. This is the connection that gave Tabitha her first job. They showed up to our meetings, band concerts and school assemblies. They were there for talent shows, and sat right next to me during the stressful court appointments. One even took my daughter's art to be professionally framed and brought gifts when she travelled internationally. They gave the kids a break from us and let them have one on one time. They loved these girls, and are a gigantic part of our villages. I also want to let the caseworkers know how important they were, and that they all did a great job fighting for the kids. For privacy reasons, I'll leave their names out, but you were the backbone to creating our new additions to our family. Thank you!

A couple of years into fostering, I began to feel like I needed to be another type of support for these kids. I am a music teacher, giving lessons out of my home. After many months of considering if I would do this, I decided to offer free music lessons for foster and adoptive families during the summer. I wanted to give these children an opportunity that they may have never been able to do. I also offered free lessons for the siblings, the biological kids. I understand that when families decide to foster, the biological kids lose opportunities as well, because the whole family schedule and energies now revolve around normalizing the foster kids into their family. I ended up teaching many different families from doing this. I chose to voluntarily give up my time, talents and energy to help build up these villages.

A couple years later, my friend who had invited people to the park thanked me for answering her "friend wanted ad". I told her I was glad she reached out. When our natural villages start tending to wane, it's important that we still have the support system to keep us going. We are still pretty excellent resources in each other's villages.

So here is my advice to you: If you want the opportunity to serve foster families and kids, then just look around. I think it's totally appropriate to go ahead and ask the parents what they need. If I were being honest, a few responses that I may have answered would probably have been: bring me a milkshake or candy bar, donate to angel trees or toys for tots, offer to watch my kids while I take a nap, talk to my foster kids like they are real people who deserve respect, invite them to birthday parties, give us hand me down clothes, stand with me and keep me in real conversation as I am doing the dishes. Love us. Don't forget about us. Being a parent is a 24/7 job. So is parenting someone else's children. It is rare that we get a break or even validation. Don't give us dirty look in the store, or ask how much money we get paid. Don't forget about us. Our heart are heavy and so are the hearts of these fragile traumatized kids. We are doing the best we can. It's like what Plato taught us, "Be kind, for everyone you meet is fighting a hard battle".

Not everyone is called to foster or adopt, but everybody is called to do something. Keep your eyes open for opportunities to build up a village, and if you are considering being a foster parent yourself, come talk to us. There are plenty of villages that need people just like you, people who are willing to read this book and learn about my fostering journey.

Creating an Ohana: Taking some tips from a tiny Hawaiian princess

I have a very average home filled with average people who live average lives. There is nothing extraordinarily special about us, and we enjoy living this simple life. We have enough for what we need and we make sure to fill our moments with each other. I like to think that because we are a foster family, that we do have some unique traits, like being really flexible and finding new and interesting ways to serve others. I also think that we have taught ourselves to have big hearts. To some extent, it comes naturally, and in other ways, we really have to work at it. It is the same with any family and their characteristics as a whole. Some families may be great at providing adventures for the family, while others may put a lot of time and energy into extracurricular activities for the kids, such as children's musical theater, karate lessons or dance competitions. Some are wound together through strong religion. My family has some of each of these traits and goals. Some families may be really good at channeling their energies into blossoming strengths. Way to go families!

  I think that every successful family works on what keeps them strong. Successful families don't necessarily mean a typical biologically nuclear family. The family has so many different looks to it. Looking towards Disney for a little insight, we are reminded of a story about what it takes to be a family, or Ohana, as it is called in Lilo and Stitch. These two sisters had to learn to take the remaining pieces of their family and reassemble the best they could after their parents had died in a tragic car accident, leaving Nani as the legal guardian. During the struggle of adjusting to living on their own, the 19-year-old older sister Nani, works every minute to try to provide them with just the basics. At one point, six-year-old Lilo is finally able to confront her role in her own life and asks if they are a broken family. Can you imagine how much that would have shattered her sister's heart? She tries to shimmy herself into the parent role for her little sister, but doesn't have the right knowledge and skills to make it work yet. She tried to deny it at first, then admits that it's a true statement. Lilo is a handful for her sister, being full of adventurous life and sass, but- she is still just a little girl. She has an active mind and sees things in a way that Nani can't. Nani is so overwhelmed by life and stepping into adulthood before she was ready, that she doesn't have the mental energy to let her imagination loose on adventures like her sister would. At this point, this family was not successful, and it wasn't really set up to be that way. Teenagers are just little adults in training, and are not yet intended to be the sole caretakers of young children, which is why it was so hard for Nani.

  Although there were several missing pieces from the Pelekai family, one thing that was not missing was the bond between the sisters. It was seen throughout the movies and was one of the things that kept the family going. However, one major hurdle was the lack of a support system. When the family is strong enough, you can use each other as supports, but when it is so fragile like this example, one late payment or bad inspection could have separated them indefinitely. There was a caseworker that came to check up on the girls during the movie, but I wouldn't call him a support in any way. When simple parenting techniques or leads on more secure jobs could have been the stepping stone that was needed to get Nani more stable, she was left every time with glares and threats from the notorious Mr. Bubbles. Lilo spent much of her time acting out and living in a distorted version of reality. Having a better support system could have helped in a big way. In the state that I live in, there are so many resources for struggling families, including parenting classes, free lunch programs in the summer and even free respite care to give parents, or caregivers, a break both mentally and physically. I can't imagine that only my area of the United States has these kinds of excellent free resources, all of which come without the state intervening in the court ordered process. They needed help and resources to be successful. Perhaps if Nani could have found a local mom in the neighborhood who also had young kids, she could have traded babysitting for each other. She could have used the extra support from people who surrounded her to get the help that she had needed to keep a steady job. Social connections are a great way to keep your goal in focus.

Family ties get enhanced by *choosing* to spend time with each other. When told that a family activity is happening, we don't always see the kids running out the door and hopping into the car as enthusiastically as we would like. It will often take some convincing or perhaps an enticing promise that there will be something in it for them in return for a good attitude. When we do find that everyone in the family is eager for the outing, geared up with positive attitudes and an exploratory spirit, that is when we find that we get the most bonding time out of it. My own kids are always, I mean ALWAYS ready for a one on one outing. They get the chance to feel affection just for them, and the attitudes are often stellar. They get the opportunity to choose the activity we do for our alone time. We call them either dates or adventures. Creating wholesome activities will not only help them feel closer to you and your family in the present, but it will also give you and your family the memories of the escapades that will sometimes last an entire lifetime. These adventures don't have to be fancy or ultra-spectacular, but giving of your time can be one of the most sacred gifts of all. Failure to act on these opportunities when they are presented to us, can leave cracks in our relationships. Bonding experiences will stay with us so that when we are able to open up our memories of our most cherished times, they most likely will be with our families.

Another characteristic of building a strong family is respect. Not just one-sided respect, but mutual respect. Lilo, although only six years old, didn't have much respect in the relationship. She was always getting herself into trouble and at first couldn't see her sister as a guardian, or even as someone to protect and watch over her. There is a part of the movie where the social worker is making an unexpected visit to the home, and everything seems to be going wrong, from the stove cooking something disgusting, to the child being left home with all the doors locked. Mr. Bubbles starts questioning Lilo about how things are going at home. You can see Nani in the background trying to coach her to say the right things. Nani is desperate to ensure that they say the exact correct phrases because she has fear that saying the wrong thing might get Lilo taken away. She's not wrong. So Lilo recites them as if she has the list memorized for her monthly visit. When asked if she is happy she responds just how she had rehearsed, with a little embellishment at the end that made her sister flinch. It's no wonder that there was concern when Lilo was playing with Voodoo dolls and whispering how she had no friends. Lilo doesn't have those same fears about being taken away that Nani has for her, which makes sense, since a kid that age wouldn't have the same life experience that her sister would have. Not taking the questioning seriously, Nani in horror rushes to try to remedy the situation. She mentions that there have already been several caseworkers. Mr. Bubbles lets her know that he is the one that people call when things go wrong, and things have indeed gone wrong.

There is so much packed into this minute of the movie. When a child is placed in the home, the caseworker will often come by up to three times during the first week. They do have certain quotas that they have to meet, for everybody's safety. When things settle down, we had them in our home just once a month. When things were a little trickier, we would see that they started bringing extra support. When things do start going wrong, you start seeing a lot of new people, hence the Mr. Bubbles character in the movie. We did see a lot of caseworkers leave. Typically they will train the newbies who are taking their places. The burnout among caseworkers is staggeringly high. Every month we would have the same visit. The caseworker would come, and the younger foster kids loved entertaining them. The older foster kids either hated, loved or tolerated the visits, depending on how mad they were at the system.

The ears of the caseworkers were always ready to hear any hint of a problem that they could put into their notes. After they take the kids, one by one in private, into the bedrooms to interview them, then as they emerged from the private interview they bring the issues to us. We just smile and nod as they explain the many things that we are doing horribly wrong. For example, that we feed them too many servings of fresh produce a day, or maybe one had a nightmare a few weeks before or they can't always find clean socks. We promise to try to do better and they write it down in their notes. One time a caseworker fought us on forcing us to require them to bring a water bottle to bed. We spent a good fifteen minutes explaining that they have been spilling the water because they don't keep the lid on, and it soaks into the mattress when it tips over, along with the urine from the accidents that the kids now have because they drink at all hours of the night. We tried to explain that the water would drip down the bunkbed and it had stained the wood, but no one wanted to really hear our version, they just had to make sure that they were jotting down enough notes in their binder to write the report. We once had to be called into the therapy session because one of the kids didn't like our special sauce that we used in our stir fry vegetable and told the caseworker that our food was making him sick- so we have to stop using the sauce. Olive Oil. We have to ban olive oil from our kitchen, which ended up making him mad because we then couldn't use it when making our French fries, fried chicken or any of the meats that we cooked. Then we had to have another meeting where we got into trouble for not cooking the food to be tasty enough for him because we couldn't use the oil anymore. The point is, these caseworkers really do listen to the kids, and if you have a good one, they will be heard. Maybe we will be heard too. Even if we do have to hear about trivial details that we need to fix for them. If Mr. Bubbles were to arrive at our house for a visit, I might have been a little nervous about how things would be taken too, even if we didn't do anything wrong. Just being on the other side of the system is always a little nerve wracking.

  There is still some fear in Lilo, even though she doesn't understand everything. I was sitting with one of my adopted daughters during one scene of the movie and she was shocked to realize that she had the same conversation that was happening in the movie. In a moment of exasperation, her mom had yelled at her "if you don't stop being bad you are going to be taken away! And it will be your fault." She was just a young girl when she heard those words used against her. Years later, that is exactly what happened, as she was removed from her house. Although it was not her fault, the words will forever ring through her ears. When the alien Stitch was introduced to the movie, he also had to figure out how to fit in with the family. He bonded with the young girl right away, but was not as accepted by anyone else. They created a bond that got them through the really hard times. Stitch talked about how he found his own family all on his own, and how good it was for him. One of the most important concepts of the movie is that you can create your own ohana, and it doesn't matter how new you are to each other. You can still be family for each other. We know that the definition of ohana deals with two concepts of everyone staying together and you will always be remembered, as part of the family. Even with so many people that have come into our home to be a part of our family, they are never forgotten, and I remember everyone that leaves.

The "alien experiment" that came to visit was naturally destructive, because he was created that way. It didn't take him long at all to realize that there were different kinds of people around him. Little Lilo even in her young years commented on his destructiveness and suggested to him to channel that energy into something else. Build instead of destroy, she encouraged. This also relates to so many children I have seen in the system. We are the ones that are trying to divert their destructive intentions and let them see that there really is good inside of themselves. They don't always see it, in fact, they may not even know that they are being destructive at all. So much of it comes naturally to them, and they can't always be in control of their actions. There will be learning opportunities, and teaching moments every day because of this. That is the nice way to say that it will be hard, and you will struggle. They are worth it, always remind yourself of that. We all have our Stitches in our lives.

Do you notice how savvy the young girl is in the movie? You would never guess that she is only six, and of course that may just be a writer's style. She thinks through things more than that average six-year-old. She was even so in tune to the elements around her that she was convinced that bringing a peanut butter sandwich to a fish could affect the weather. If she seemed smarter than normal for her age, it's likely due to the traumas she has experienced. Foster children are commonly very self-aware about their environment. I had a boy who would know exactly how many cars drove by our house, and was always watching every person around him. It was definitely bordering on annoying for us, because he was able to interject himself into every single private conversation we were trying to have. It took us a few months to realize that he was doing this because it was a survival instinct, called hyper-awareness. He had honed in on this instinct at a young age because that is what he needed to stay safe. He was from a dangerous, manipulative and abusive environment. Just like Lilo, he used his awareness of his environment to stay safe.

 In the end, Nani, Lilo and Stitch were sanctioned as a family, fully accepting of each other and willing to stay together leaving no one behind. It was not easy for them in the beginning to automatically love each other. The same may be true for fostering. Although there is love there, it doesn't typically come on the first day. There will be some love that you can give them right away, because you chose to be a foster family, and knew that you had love to give a child. You may not be all the way in love however. Just as a dating relationship, it takes nurturing and time to create love. It was a roller coaster of emotions for our family to make it to adoption day, and it was hard work. We love this Hawaiian example of family-ohana. Both of my brothers lived in Hawaii, and my sister-in-law came to be part of our family when she lived there as well. Creating a family is kind of like being on Hawaii time. Relax, enjoy the waves, listen to some Elvis on the beach, and wait for your family to come together. It will happen. With patience, time and love, we created our ohana.

Mirror, Mirror On the Wall:
Why can't I see myself at all?

One of our foster kids came from a broken and dysfunctional family. Her own mother, according to her, had told her she was a mistake, ugly and stupid. She was told that she wasn't wanted, and that everything was her fault. When you are told this even a couple times you may start to believe it. Well, guess what? That's the definition of emotional abuse, being told something consistently to put you down and make you feel worthless. How long will it take someone to recover who was told their whole life that they were not wanted? Probably a lifetime, if it ever completely happens. Her therapists did not do a good enough job in her opinion of helping her cope with this. So that's where we swoop in.

We decided to grab our phone and put on a song about loving herself every time she started to say something negative about who she was. It didn't take long for her to start to break the habit. I hope she can realize that we want her to see how beautiful she is. In case she needs a little encouragement, here it is. We spent a good year trying to put good thoughts into her head about herself but she just couldn't hear them. She looked in the mirror and saw an ugly person who will never measure up. When we look at the same mirror, we see a beautiful, smart and talented young woman who has all the potential in the world to become anything she wants. I don't make this up and I'm not just trying to bolster her self-esteem. I'm just telling her what I see and know to be true.

Seeing her beauty

Every once in a while, she will come bursting into a room and proclaim "I have great hair today!!!!" We follow up with, "You work hard on your hair and it looks great every day." She rolls her eyes and tells us that we are supposed to say that. I tell her back that I must be doing a good job then, but that doesn't change the fact that she still does have great hair all the time. Other days she will put herself down, and tell us negative things about herself, like maybe her hair looks weird. Sometimes it is just too easy to focus on the negative mindset.

Soon after the adoption we told her that she was free to put herself down, but it is not going to do herself any favors. I ask my kids if they would say the things that they say about themselves to other people. No, they always say. "Why would we talk bad about other people?" It only takes tiny thoughts to seep into our minds and can discourage us. It doesn't matter if you put yourself down a little or a lot. It is still a put down and she doesn't deserve it. I always tell her that she wouldn't want her friends or family talking about her the way that she talks to herself. It would be hurtful. She is my daughter so I don't think even she should be allowed to talk be any of my kids this way. My other four kids don't struggle with this. They have all of the self-esteem in the world, as they should.

Seeing her talents

When she started high school she went to her Seminary class, which is a religion class that they can attend during the school day. On the first day of class the instructor asked if anyone played the piano. <Cricket cricket> No one. Then he asked if anyone had access to a free piano teacher. She perked up and said that her mom is a piano teacher. He told her to go home and learn to play the piano. So she came home after having a wonderful first day of high school and sat down at the piano. I assured her that her clarinet history and sharp mind would let her pick up the music right away. I assisted very little, but she was able to figure out a whole hymn on the first day. She was bouncing with excitement. I wasn't shocked at all. I just smiled and told her I knew she could do it. She spent the next weeks at the piano and learned new songs every day. She was brave enough to put herself in front of the seminary class and play for them. This would not have happened a few years before or even a few months before. In the past even if she thought she had the ability to play, her self-proclaimed awkwardness would have held her back. Within a few weeks, she could play any song with a little practice, and now she sits at the piano and can teach herself anything. I can't wait until she gets to accompany me when I play the other instruments. Not anymore, even in a room full of strangers. She is starting to see the real image in the mirror.

Seeing her scars

Both figuratively and physically we all have scars. For her, she had both that were plainly visible. These are shown in the mirror that we all see. When she looks at the mirror, she sees so much etching and too many cracks to fully see her reflection. Maybe she is self-conscious, or maybe with her healing, she doesn't notice them as much anymore. They are a reminder of where she has been and where she is headed. This is the advice that she got from a musician that she deeply admires, when we saw him in person. Some of these are never going to go away. With time and lots of love, our goal is to clean the mirror and diminish the etches as much as we can. She needs to see a full view of herself as she really is. I imagine that the mirror that God sees her out of contains no blemishes. It is bright and clear, and you can see the beauty that shines both inside and outside.

Seeing her potential

When we first met this girl, I have to admit, I couldn't tell what path she was going to take. Usually I have a pretty good instinct for telling how people are going to turn out. I can say pretty confidently, "Watch out for this one friend, she is going to stab you in the back." It doesn't take long before we start to see it happen. Other times it's more like, "That kid is going to make it into any college he applies to." When I looked at my own daughter at first it was so unclear. Even my view of her mirror was blurry and scuffed up a little. Every day we were able to take off a little bit of the blurriness and see what was underneath. It can get me emotional to see who much potential she is making.

When she was in the 8th grade band, her band teachers showed a lot of interest in her, even though they kept putting her in a third clarinet seat. Once she moved to second clarinet for a week or so, but then got bumped down. She was discouraged, but I was thrilled. I didn't see it as a downgrade. I saw it as for the first time, they could see a girl with talent as I did. I told her that they could see the potential. She got a lot of attention from them, and many compliments. It never made sense that they would complement her but keep her at the bottom. She was able to stay focused and not loose too much heart. Around springtime of that year, the high school had started recruiting. Her goal was to make it into the beginning band, even if she was the last clarinet player she would be happy that she was able to play. I told her that I could see clearly that she would get in the highest band that a freshman could get into. She had no faith in this process at first. Then she saw the scales and songs required to audition. The chromatic scales intimidated her a lot. I sat down at the piano and gave her a few theory lessons. Again, she was shocked when she had the scale down within about 48 hours. Once she saw that she could do it, her talent started to explode. She was able to help other students and sight-read music the day that it was handed out. Even though I am a mama bear who is not afraid to poke my head into a situation to make sure that the teachers understand the back story, I never had to do that with band. I knew that this was something she could excel in on her own.

When the auditions came, she was really surprised and concerned that she was one of the only ones that was auditioning for the clarinet. Even one of her best friends decided that she wouldn't pursue band. Thinking that she must be foolish for trying to press forward, she got very nervous during her recording that she knew the band teacher would be listening to and scrutinizing. According to her, she BOMBED the audition. It was bad, like she should hide her face in shame bad. She was embarrassed to show her face around her teachers. It was to be posted that Friday if they had made the band. One Tuesday of the same week, she noticed the high school and middle school band teachers talking in the office and heard her name. She ducked down under the glass and tried to hear what they were saying about her. That didn't work, so she just went on her way and wondered what they were saying. The next day her teacher asked her to resubmit her audition because they wanted to hear her play again. She came home and practiced all day. By the second time she recorded, she had it mastered. Her nerves were gone and she just did her best, just like what I knew she could do. By Thursday she was pulled aside and told that she had made it to the advanced band! She wasn't to tell anyone else yet because they weren't posting it until the next day.

I was thrilled when she ran to the car to tell me her news as I was picking her up from school that day. It was my pleasure to tell her that her band teachers no longer saw potential in her anymore. They saw the actual progress, the end result. She thought about that for a few days before she came back and said she understood what I was saying. They no longer had to hope that she would grow into the potential that others saw in her. She was already living it herself. Once she had surpassed the apparent expectation that people had for her, we aren't allowed to call it potential anymore. It just becomes who you are. People expect great things from her and she can see it now. It doesn't discourage her anymore, because she has become someone stronger and more powerful than she ever thought that she would be able to be! The glass clears up even more.

Seeing her future

One night when she was 14 she came into our room and told us all about her dreamhouse. She actively danced around the room ecstatically laying out a virtual tour for our minds to go on. She had everything lined out, starting with the color and exact wood of her front door. She visually painted for us the types of French doors and the breakfast nook overlooking her garden. She described the type of mirror she could have and the layout of every room. She broadened her arms as she described how big her master bedroom would be. She would have a huge bathroom and walk in closet. The bed would be carved from wood and have her and her husband's names wood burned into it with her kids' names. My husband asked where the messy kids are going to go, if there would be a place for them. She described the mud room, and the art and music rooms in the basement. She will design their rooms around their personalities, but she doesn't know what they will be like yet, so she will have to wait and see. She talked a million miles an hour and her eyes gleamed with light from her dream. Where did this dreamer come from? She has never expressed her dreams before.

I joked that she better be hanging out in a medical library if she was going to find and marry someone that rich. She laughed and thought that was a good idea, and I had to remind her that I was only joking. At the end of the tour, she came back to reality and said "Anyway, that's just my dream. It doesn't mean it will happen." My husband looked at her and said "All of my dreams came true. I live in Utah, married Sarah and have great kids. I have everything I dreamed of." I reminded him about the fact that he would love to raise horses and goats again. He said that the time will come for that later, he is busy raising and enjoying kids right now.

Until this moment, she had been terrified of the thought that someday she might have kids. She said at one point that she may just end up adopting a baby. A few weeks before the adoption I explained to her that it was okay if she wasn't fully attached to us yet. We were ready for her to be part of our family forever and I had enough faith for both of us. I also let her know that it was okay if she thought at this point in her life that she may not be fully attached to a future partner. She just needs to know that attachment is a tricky thing in her situation. We don't take it personally if she doesn't know how connected she will be to anyone. It will come in time. It may be a slow process to learn to love and trust someone with your heart. So for her to announce that someday she would like a nice house with a husband and children is another milestone in her life journey. She even has a name picked out of her daughter, and it's a beautiful one.

Seeing life after high school

Middle school and elementary school were no less than horrible for her. She was bullied, thought she was worthless and stupid. I told her that she just had to get past middle school because she is going to LOVE high school. She was nervous the first couple of days, but she mastered it in no time at all. She was able to branch out and start hanging out with different kinds of people. She discovered her love of French and pep band was her savior.

A few months after she moved in with us, she began to see that maybe there was a possibility that she could actually get some kind of education and she mentioned living at home. I joke with all of my kids that they can stay here as long as they want and I will build them a guest house in the backyard. She said she will probably live there for a long time. Fine with me, I said. Eventually "education" turned into Southern Utah University, the local school that I had graduated from. After her adoption, the local school started to turn into the Biggest school in the state- BYU. It is a lofty goal. One that I don't know how we can support without hefty amounts of financial aid. Even then, who knows. Now when we mention the guest house, she tries to say in a nice sensitive way, that she may not actually live in the guest house after all. She was trying not to hurt my feelings since her dreams were growing! She plans on leaving sooner than we had talked about. I smiled on the inside. Not because I want her to leave. Not at all, I would be fine with them staying as long as they wanted to (Yes, I know that answer will change in about a decade). For now, she is already dreaming too big for our house, and that is just how it should be.

Her mirror is starting to look awfully clear at this point. She can see that she really is all of the things that we see in her. She is brilliant, amazing and a survivor of her old scratched up mirror. Every time that we are ready to pull out our Love Yourself song, she catches herself and can actually give herself a compliment instead.

Seeing herself

She was hanging out with us about the time that she would normally get to bed on a school night. She was checking her school account and realized that she had an assignment due the next day. As she announced this, she bolted out of the room to hurry and finish her homework before she passes out from tiredness. She came in proud of herself a few moments later and announced, "I'm a GOOD GIRL! I already had finished my homework!" I decided to try a little sarcasm, which she is learning to take. Usually it is like walking on eggshells around her. Any little thing could trigger the self-hating thoughts. So I said, "Oh good, I'm glad you are not a BAD girl for not finishing your homework!" It took her a moment and then she shot back- "NOPE! I would be a good girl if I had my homework done. I would be a good girl if I had *not* had my homework done." And the crowd went wild! I could hear the imaginary cheering of the stadium in my head. She gets it! Another milestone! Self-love! We were so excited that she has this new self-awareness. She yelled "Night! I'm out of here!", shut the door and ran off to get ready for bed. High fives all around. She can see herself in the mirror in a new way.

Seeing yourself as an 8-cow wife

There is a religious video that I used to watch as a kid. A young girl named Mahana was the "ugly girl" of her small island village. Even her own father was embarrassed by her. When it came time to barter for her daughter's marriage, the father had little faith that he would get any cows, which was the custom. Women were defined by their amount of cows that they would receive, and that was their worth. Some were deemed worthy of just 2 cows, and the really fancy and beautiful wives got 4 or 5 cows. The dad proposed 3 cows, but the suitor proclaimed that three cows was not going to be enough for her. Nobody took him seriously because they were in such shock at the statement. On the day of the marriage, Johnny Lingo, the husband to be, showed up with 8 cows! No one quite understood. They took off and he later gifted her a beautiful mirror, made of the finest materials, so that she could see how beautiful she was. Months later, when they returned to the island, there was a change in her. Suddenly she was stunningly beautiful and her smile lit up the room. How had she changed? No one quite understood. Johnny Lingo explained that he had always seen her beauty and had loved her since they were young children. It didn't matter if no one else could see what he saw. He could see her reflection as something that no one else could. They could only see the scratches and stains. When questioned, he explained that a person's true worth had nothing to do with what people saw, but only as one truly is. He had made the best bargain of all, a few cows for the women that he loved. He could see the worth of who she was, and when she was able to see it too, her whole countenance changed. This world, especially the American society, would be so different if the people could see their own self-worth. I think we are all pretty amazing.

Cleaning the mirror

I don't know if her mirror will ever be as clean as she wants it to be. I doubt we will ever look at the same mirror and see the same image. That's why we have different perspectives. Imagine what it would be like if we all saw everything exactly the way that it was. There would be no potential. Or change. Or choice about who you would become. Tabitha talks sometimes of going into massage therapy, or being a doctor, or some other way to help others. If I were to tell her that she was destined to a life as a janitor, she may believe it. I love that she has opinions, and she knows that she matters. In our family and in the world, she matters.

Miracles everywhere!

Let's talk about the miracles. There are just so many great things that have come out of foster care. These are just a couple of the miracles that I have seen. More hare happening every day.

The miracle of a movie

In a remake of the classic movie Annie, one of my favorite movies, a young foster girl gets up in front of a large fundraiser and sings a beautiful song about the different opportunities that have changed her life. I listen to this song all the time on my playlist. The song delicately talks about how she doesn't need to be nervous because she can see that people are smiling at her. She can't believe that she is allowed the chance to do something amazing. She sees that if she were to take that chance that she had never been allowed before, then her dreams would start to come true. The girl recognizes that this is a changing point for her because of the opportunities that she is being given, and she soars. This song is one of my favorites. She was able to feel the comfort of the people smiling at her and share what she was feeling. Look at me! She has knowledge of her worth and is ready to spread it to others. When we foster, we are giving them the opportunities that they didn't have before. When we watch what they transform into because of the opportunities, it is life changing! This movie came out into theaters when I was waiting for my first foster placement. I left the movie in tears and ready to take in the first child that was needing a home. I vowed to make it possible for these kids to dream and flourish. It was only about a week later that I got the call and was able to start my fostering journey.

The miracle of a talent show

I kept this sentiment in my heart while helping these kids. A few years later when I was fostering Emma at the time, I got to witness one of these moments. She came to live with us in November, and a few months later we had a school talent show. Lyla who was six back then was going to play a song on the piano and she practiced all the time. It was fun and she learned the music easily. My other daughter announced with just a few weeks' notice, that she wanted to also learn the piano to play in front of the whole school. I had maybe, MAYBE, a month's notice. Maybe less. I had been telling her I wouldn't start teaching her lessons until I knew that she could commit to practicing every day before school, like her sister. What you need to know about her is that he has no inhibitions. She is one of the bravest kids I have ever met. She could put a one-man variety show on for the school for an hour and still not run out of material. The problem was she had never played the piano before. Quite frankly, she had no inkling of musical talent at all. As a piano teacher, I wracked my brain and came up with a way that she would be able to learn the song The Rose. She said it was one of her mom's favorite songs. It took a lot of patience for both of us to work so closely together on the piano bench, but night after night we worked one note at a time. We learned to work in unison and I provided the chords of the song as she learned the melody. She rarely got discouraged, and spent every spare moment learning just a few lines of the song. This was a true challenge for her. She struggled in every subject in school, and teaching her even one spelling word could take her a whole day. We finally made it to the audition day and played it together for the teachers. She messed up many times and had to start over. The teachers were very nice about it and told her that she still had a week to work on it before the talent show. They were showing their faith that she might get a little better.

They day of the talent show came, Valentine's Day. She wore a beautiful dress and danced up and down the line where the other kids in the talent show were quietly waiting. I show up about 15 minutes early and check in on her to see if she is nervous. Her therapist warned me that she may back out. Not surprisingly, she is bouncing off the walls, as excited as can be. She is running to every person coming in the room, hugging teachers, hopping on the stage etc., she is so hyper I finally have to tell her to stay in the line. I jokingly asked her if she knew everyone in the room. She looked around and said "yep". And I believe she really did.

My younger daughter had composed her own song, at age 6, and performed it perfectly. I was very proud of her. As the show starts, I am so happy to see so many talented young people. They were all so brave and worked hard. Several were my former music students. I have to admit that I didn't know what to expect from my foster daughter. Half way through the talent show she started looking for her mom in the audience. She was nowhere to be found. I had told the caseworker to invite her and I have personally told her the date, time and location of the talent show. Her face fell as she realized that her mom was not going to show up, again. It was often the case. When my girl is next in line, I go up to her to check on her. She was shaking and had big tears in her eyes. She was nervous. I didn't have much time to comfort her, so I just put my arm around her and we went to the piano. I helped her put her hands in the right place and have her breathe for a second before she started. Her nerves got to her and she messed up on a few notes. She says, "I messed up." I said, "I don't care, you are doing great!" And I pointed out her notes on the page and talked her through it step by step. She did mess up on several notes, but you know the cool thing? She kept going. It even kind of sounded like she was just embellishing the notes a little bit.

"You can do it…you are doing great…it's ok if you mess up, just keep *going…I am so proud of you.*"

These are the words that I was whispering to her. Then from behind me I started to hear sniffing. The teachers were crying from where they were watching. That got me going, but then my heart swelled up and I felt so much pride for her. My eyes even got a tiny bit teary, which is somewhat uncommon for me. She was incredible! She was doing it, and people were finally able to see this miracle right in front of me. One of her dreams was becoming true and it was turning into an amazing opportunity for her.

As she finished, Emma stood up and gave me a hug. Then she whispers, "Today I am the proudest person in the world for me. I have never been stronger than today." And I told her I was also the proudest person in the world for her. Now others watching this simple talent will not have known her history, or how many hours she put into learning that song. When I turned around I finally saw all of the tears from the people that have worked so hard to protect and teach my daughter. Some of these teachers are the reason that she was with me. They stood up for her safety and made sure that she was placed in a home. They saw her taking the opportunity and soaring. They knew where she had come from and knew that this was an amazing feat. To this day she still talks about The Rose and plays it, or rather stumbles through it, whenever someone new comes to the house. She continued to learn the piano, as best as she could, but her brain just isn't really wired for that. There are so many connections that are made in music which make it a monumental struggle for her. That's not the point though. It's not that she wanted to be a concert pianist. She just wanted to be able to work hard enough to play a song that her mom loves. She has touched so many people, and I'm told every time I walk into the school how different she has been since this change was made. She has so much potential that she has no idea about. She is truly changing lives with her sweet spirit, and she is not only thriving-she is soaring. She met her goal with flying colors. She is one of my favorite miracles, and I am so glad that I got to be there to witness her special defining moment. This girl has changed my world.

The miracle of looking into the future

One night as we were getting ready for bed, Emma, who was still about eight at the time was watching me as she peaked out from the top of her bunk bed. She had been with us about two months. I liked to sit at the grand piano in the middle of the house where the kids could hear me play as they drifted off the sleep. I remember liking that when I was a kid, so I try to do it often for them as well. I could see her watching me so when I finished a song I went to go have a good night reassuring talk with her, which was the nightly norm. She was pondering what it would be like to drive a car. We did the math and figured she would be learning it just seven short years. I could see the real question behind her eyes. Would she ever be able to get to learn to drive if she was still in foster care? Where was she even going to be living seven years into the future? Here is how the conversation started to go:

Emma: "Well…I'm just wondering…"

Me: "Who will get to teach you to drive when you are older?"

Emma: Nods with big eyes.

Me: "I wish I knew. I wish I could tell you all of the answers that you want to know. I'm not sure how long we get to have you in our home, but I know I am going to love every minute that you are here with us."

Emma: "…What if…YOU get to teach me?"

Me: "I would love that. It's hard to know how long you get to stay here."

Emma: "What if…" and her eyes got bigger and brighter with hope, "I get to stay here FOREVER?"

Me: Heart melting

Emma: Heart melting

Me: "Then I would be the luckiest mom in the world."

Emma: "AWWW!"

This was another miracle in my life. The moment that she was able to see that she may be staying with us permanently. It had to have been such a bittersweet moment for her. Opening up her heart to me might mean that she has to close the idea of going home with her mom. It was a long seventeen months later, but I was floating on air the day that we got to officially adopt her.

The miracle of superglue

There is another Emma miracle that I love to relive. We were walking to the school bus, all of the kids singing and skipping as we made our daily walk. She gets silent and out of nowhere she says one of the most profound things I have ever heard from her, "I used to have a lot of tiny cracks in my heart. You guys are picking up the pieces and super gluing it back together." Nothing can really prepare you for the emotions that can come from hearing something like this. This is when you feel your heart grow a little bigger. You fight back tears which is hard to do as the winter chill of the air already stings them. This is not something that she would normally come out of her mouth. It is the moments like this that keep you going through the hard parts of fostering. As much as we are going through, I can't imagine the raw emotions that they carry inside of them.

The miracle of a good teenager

I once had two boys, around the ages of nine and eleven. They were such a joy to have. They actually came to stay with us multiple times, and it was so much fun. They were very well adjusted and had a great relationship with their parents. They loved our kids and got along really well with our foster daughter. The three of them spent a good week choreographing a dance for us. They practiced a couple hours a day. It was a meaningful song because it was a tribute to Paul Walker who had recently passed away from a car crash. He was from a series of car racing movies that we all enjoyed, so hearing the song was sentimental for all of us. The night before they headed back home, we finally got to watch them perform it for us in a little talent show that the kids threw for us. We recorded it and love to go back and watch it. The kids worked so hard and their faces glowed with the triumph that they felt as they finished their tribute. I loved being part of this moment. The joy that they had as they showed us their hard work will always bring a smile to my face. This is the attitude that these boys always had. They came back a few months later and we had a great reunion of sorts. I would see them around town on and off until eventually I found out that they moved to Florida. I was happy for them, but sad for myself and kids because a tiny part of our family was far away. Several years later, my foster mom heart jumped for joy when we saw them at the swimming pool a few months after our own adoption. They had also been adopted by family and were just visiting their dad here in town. They were so happy, like always. I got to witness their happily ever after.

    The first time we fostered teenagers, we were just a stopping point for them. They were only with us about a week. Another set of brothers, also two years apart. The oldest one was seventeen and a half, about to leave the system in just a couple of months. The foster family that housed them were burned out and had finally had enough. They had been fostering for several decades and were getting older, and ready to be empty nesters. We offered to have the boys came with us while they were getting their next foster family ready. We were just doing short term fostering at the time because we had a baby and another foster daughter. We enjoy doing short term, because it's more like a slumber party for the kids and we are able to give a break to the other foster families. This older boy wanted to go to a bonfire in the mountains with some friends, including his girlfriend. He wanted my permission. This was my first experience with parenting any teenager, so I knew I had to pick my words carefully. I sat him down on the couch and we talked about the pros and cons of having him go. I could tell that where he used to live, he had as much freedom as he wanted, because the parents were just tired of having them around. Our talk revolved around what would happen if there was alcohol at the party. I asked if he would be targeted in any way because he was a foster kid and almost eighteen. He said he would and it was not fair. I was able to teach him about being in the right place at the right time.

We set up a plan for the night. He was going to be allowed to go there on his own, since he had a job and his own car. I knew there wouldn't be any cell reception, so I wanted him to text me at 10:30 on his way back. The campsite was only fifteen minutes away, so I would be able to track him down fairly easy if I didn't hear from him by then. He was really surprised that I let him go, and told me that he wouldn't break my trust. He was able to follow all of the instructions and made it home with plenty of time. He was driving out of the campsite when the sheriffs were coming around to check in on all of the teenagers. It is likely that nothing would have happened if he had stayed longer because he said there was no alcohol, but he was relieved that he didn't even have to be in a situation where law enforcement was checking in on them.

The next day I had to let them know that their belongings were being packed up at their home and would be waiting for them when they were done staying with us. It was really hard to tell them that because I don't think I was the right person to give them the news. They just shrugged and said that it had happened before. The younger of the boys didn't really talk or eat while he was with us. I haven't heard from him since, but they did give permission to add their names to our foster care wall. The older boy thanked me for letting them stay there and told me I was doing a good job. I checked in on him about a year later, and it did my soul good to hear that he was enrolled in a University. He had received grants and scholarships and was majoring in something that he loved. He proudly reported that he did not get lost in the system, and he was doing excellent. He is one of my success stories, even though I wasn't really part of his story, and he may not remember me in the future, he became part of mine.

The miracle of Andy Biersack

I have also been able to be the giver of miracles. When Tabitha came to live with us, she hid in her room for several days. Her lifeline was music, and a specific kind of music. Black Veil Brides ran through her blood. It was her version of the Backstreet Boys from my own teenage years. It was something that was so important to her, that she didn't think we would understand. The lyrics of the music were so powerful to her that she credits it for saving her life, which may very well be true. In her mind, the biggest miracle that could have come into her life would have been to meet the lead singer Andy Black. She adored him and everything he stood for. Soon after she came to live with us, she found out that the band would be at Warped Tour in Salt Lake City, just four hours north of us. She obsessed over this. It worried me because I didn't know what this kind of music stood for and the impact that it was really having. The caseworker would start to make little promises of looking into getting her tickets. At a team meeting she was told that if she got her grades up, then they would consider letting her go. The wheels were already turning in my head at this point. They talked of the different people that might be able to go with her to the concert. It wasn't just one concert, but about 50 bands rotating throughout the event center throughout the day. By some miracle, she ended up getting her grades to pass, and the day that they told her she would be allowed to go, was the day that I finally saw the real girl hiding inside. For the first time in all the time I had known her, she was happy. I saw light in her that hadn't been there before.

It was that point that I decided I would do anything I needed to in order to take her to the concert. That night I bought two tickets to Warped Tour, scared out of my mind because it was not something I would ever have done on my own. I also bought meet and greet tickets to see Andy. This was a reality and a truth in her life, she was on her way to see Andy. She talked of nothing else, and almost passed out multiple times from hyperventilating in the coming weeks, but we made it to June 24th 2017. I went with her and took her to the concert. It was full with tens of thousands of people, most with colored hair and tattoos. There were people drinking alcohol and vaping everywhere. Not to worry, the mama bear was right there. Trying to fit in with the only clothes that I could find that would not make me stand out too much. Didn't work. Her focus was clear, she could look past all of that. Andy's band was the final band that day, so we waited around for ten hours to hear him, as they did not let us leave the park. The meet and greet was incredible for both of us. I could see what she saw in him. She had picked someone to idolize who knew what he stood for. He had some issues with alcohol earlier in life, and had since sworn it off. He didn't like who he had become, so he changed himself. He writes his music for himself, and not for anyone else. One girl talked about the scars on her body, and his advice was to see the scars as something from your past. Move on past them and be proud of the progress that you have made. His whole concept is to be proud to be who you are, which is something that all the teenagers out there need to know. His concert was really fun too. The crowd that came all understood the concepts that he sang about.

  This day was a dream come true for Tabitha, and was one of the biggest miracles that will ever happen in her life. She still talks about that day. On my end, it was something so simple, spending a day with my daughter and doing something that interest her. But for her, it was something that would have never been possible if it weren't for me. I know this because she tells it to me often. I later got her Black Veil Bride tickets to see the whole band, and she swears he pointed at her in the concert and recognized her mouthing the words 'warped tour' which was seven months before. I like to think that's what happened. I do know that she has several videos of him looking and singing right at her. We were able to go again to see them at the next Warped Tour, but it didn't mean as much. She even stood right next to him and asked him a question, and although she did freak out about that, she still talks about the original Warped Tour that we went to. Her original miracle. They were all bucket list items for her, but her miracle had already happened. She met, talked to and even touched Andy. She didn't wash the hand that he high fived for a long time. Her world was opened up the day she met Andy, because she was in a place she never thought she would be, and I got to be the one to deliver that miracle.

The miracle of a business owner

Girl's camp was quickly approaching. One of the kids wasn't quite sure she wanted to camp with a bunch of teenagers, especially since not all of them were so nice to her. What was girls camp exactly? Some of the coolest adventures from my teenage years. We would take a week and get in tune with where we are spiritually in the wilderness. It is for youth ages 12-18. There are certification requirements as well, like learning to tie knots, build fires and the essential skills needed for the outdoors. It's a lot like what you would expect the boy scouts do. It's also a very spiritual experience if you pay attention. I thought the best way to show her what it was like so she wouldn't be nervous, was to show her the movie that had been in theaters a couple years before, which supposedly took hundreds of stories from campers and came up with a relatable movie. I had posted on facebook that we would be watching it, and anyone who wanted to come see it could come over. Tabitha's youth leader had a bigger space that we could watch it, and offered her movie room. Then a mother of some of the youth offered her actual movie theater for our use. We were blown away. When I told Tabitha that we would have the theater to ourselves for a private party, she was speechless. She asked how it happened, and I explained it was because of her. Someone saw a way that they could bless all of us and donated something of value for us. It was for her, Tabitha, because she was important enough. No one had ever done something for her before. She couldn't comprehend that she was enough and she was worth this little miracle. We invited probably a hundred people so that they could get in on the theater fun. It was early on a Saturday, and people actually showed up! We made cinnamon rolls for everyone, and the theater owner even let us have popcorn and a drink. With only two theaters in the town, and a hefty event rental costs, we were truly blessed. It was a wonderful movie, and she had came out a different person. She had more confidence, and everyone knew it was because of her, and a business owner who was able to show generosity towards a foster child. As was the goal, she went to girls camp and didn't want to leave. It was all she talked about for months afterwards. She had even said that if she had to move back with her mom, that she would walk across town every week just so she could go back to girls camp the following year. I hope that if the movie owner runs across this story that she knows how grateful and touched we are for her generosity. If the universe is trying to balance things out, it's working. Walls were broken down, and she asked why someone would do that for her. I got the unique privilege to tell her that people care for her. It took her weeks to process this. She said nothing good has ever been done for her or because of her. And in that moment, she was able to stand a little taller, smile bigger and finally understand that she is loved.

There are miracle surrounding us all the time in foster care. These few examples are just a few that come to mind. We can be the one that brings the miracle to them, but often, they are the ones that are the miracles. Just for being who they are. I think we are all miracles.

The Impact of foster sisters

My home growing up was a safe haven for all sorts of people. I remember exchange students from Japan, teenage mothers, along with a rotation of visiting family members and it was always fun getting to know people from all walks of life. It never really felt out of place, and we had enough space, attention and food to go around. I would say that one of the most formative experiences from my childhood would be adding three sisters to the family. I am sure that my perspective of the whole experience would be vastly different than if my mom were to retell it, which I'm sure would have way more facts and details about our lives that I never noticed at the time. Looking to see the difference between what I know about my own fostering family versus what my children would say about it, I know that they don't even know a fraction of what really happens. And that's ok. I like reliving my own rose-colored glasses version for foster care, and perhaps that is what had drawn me into fostering as an adult. Without giving away more than I need to for privacy reasons, let me tell you about those years with my childhood memories from decades ago.

I don't remember any big announcement necessarily that I would be getting some new sisters. I just remember when they showed up for the first time. We were all kind of partnered up in ages. One of the girls #1, was right around the same age as my older brother, Sean's age, in fact they were about two months apart. Sister #2 was a year and a half older than me, but it always felt as if we were the same age. Then there was sister #3, who was very close to my sister who was two years younger than me. My little brother Andy was the youngest of us seven. We quickly went from a family of six to a whopping family of 9. Every day was just jam packed with learning experiences, a lot of which I gained just by watching the interactions between my parents and my sisters. I learned new phrases like *having a crush, being* a *bookworm, treating for lice, sibling rivalry, therapist, biological mom, caseworker, the system, sexual assault, and GET*

OUT OF MY FACE! Yup, I learned the last one pretty quickly. My parents joke that our family motto used to be "Charity begins at home", then morphed into "I suffer, you suffer", and landed on "GET OUT OF MY FACE!"

Talking with my mom, I learned that the decision to take in foster children was a tough one. The answer wasn't an automatic YES! It was a lot more difficult. She was finishing up her master's degree and already running her household making sure we all were equipped with piano, dance, 4-H, church activities, both boy and girl scouts, music lessons and who knows what else. I just know that a busy family found a way to make room and time for more people. My sisters were with us for almost two years. I was about seven at the time, and she would have just turned nine. I was closest to sister #2 and we did many school things together, just because our ages matched up. She was much spunkier than I was, and way more outgoing. I think my youngest kid got some of her sassy personality, because it sure didn't come from me.

My mind is a little jumbled, as are most of the early childhood memories. I will just tell a few memories that I do have. My older sister was an avid reader. I remember her being very intelligent, and because of her tall size, people often mistook her as being much older than she actually was. Her place of refuge was her bed reading novels. School wasn't her cup of tea, so it was a struggle going for her. My parents made it very clear that they expected decent grades and attendance in school. They had both gone on to get graduate degrees. She was in the sixth grade with my brother. I don't remember them interacting much. She was very kind and had a soft heart. I'm pretty sure that her spirit animal was some sort of cat, because I have distinct memories of her purring and meowing. Her 13th birthday was held at Chuck E. Cheese and we have a video of us singing Happy Birthday to her. She beamed and was so happy. Her birthday was right after Christmas, which she said was hard sometimes. People are often burned out from celebrating, and tend to forget the December birthdays. I always remember her birthday every year, because I get to remember her face and remember her sweet spirit. I don't ever remember fighting with her, but that sure doesn't mean it didn't happen. I just like to remember the good memories.

My middle sister, like I said, was pretty close in age with me. There was more contention with her, not because I didn't love her, more because our personalities were so different. She had long thick blonde hair, and it was often difficult to take care of. She would push back against my mom who was always trying to get her to brush it. She was proud of her hair, until we got the four-letter word in our home. Lice. (Don't tell my mom that I put that word in here, it would make her shudder). We were overrun with lice. I remember being called to the office after lice checks kept happening in the classroom. It disgusted my mom, and she had to deal with several rounds of it with the whole lot of us kids. It has got to be one of the biggest challenges that she went through as a foster mom. Once the lice was gone for good, we were to never mention the word again. Maybe I'm being dramatic, but from my young perspective that is what I remember. With the exit of the four-letter word from our home, also came sister #2's haircut. Once the shock wore off, she loved it. I remember being in the hallway watching her smile and singing, brushing her hair in the mirror. She looked at me and said in an omniscient voice: "The key…is short hair". I knew I was receiving really important wisdom that I needed for the rest of my life. But…what key? I didn't really know what she was telling me. An actual key? To what door? She must have seen my confused face because she had to explain what it meant. She was right. I tell that to my own kids all the time, I do have four girls after all. The coolest part of this story was that she grew up embracing salon life as an amazing hairdresser. She has also blossomed into a wonderful mother and I am very proud of how well she has done.

One Halloween we got home from some appointment and sister #2 was nowhere to be found. My mom called my neighbor and found out she was over there. My mom, slightly exasperated, brought her back home. When asked why she left without permission, she got really sad and said that she was scared to be left alone on such a scary day. This was one of my first experiences seeing that trauma can dig into you and plant fears that I wouldn't have thought of. In my mind Halloween was a fun holiday that we would rush home from school and get dressed up for. I started to pay attention at a young age and notice the things that were a little different with my sisters. They had to schedule time to go visit their mom and they had therapist meetings. I remember waiting right outside of the door while they talked about different things. My parents were often worn out, I could tell even though I was young. My mom eventually learned that there were behaviors and situations that the girls had been in, which were not disclosed to her when the state had asked her to take on the case. She asked for information on some very specific instances that might have been a deciding factor, and was told that there were no such behaviors or traumas. When the truths started coming out in therapy, my mom confronted the caseworker, who told her that they had in fact hid the truth from them. Their argument was that if she has been told everything, they probably wouldn't have taken the girls, so they lied in order to find them a home. They weighed heavily on them. The system had lied to them. The girls stayed with us though, because we were a family. There is something special about meeting these kids, you want to invest in them and do what you can to help. The traumas that they had been in before did not impact my relationships with them. I knew about them, but it made me love them even more.

All of this happened around the time that The Lion King was brand new. I remember getting the VHS tape for my 8th birthday. I knew all about the voice that played young Simba, because we had a giant poster of him above the girl's bed. Jonathon Taylor Thomas, or JTT as he was adoringly called back then. He filled much of our conversation together, and we would dance around singing the whole soundtrack. Even my dad knew who he was, because he was the middle son on the popular tv show Home Improvement, which I would watch with him until the series ended, long after the girls made their way back home. To this day when I see him on tv, I smile as I remember these sweet moments.

    We spent most days in the summer walking to the neighborhood pool. We were actively involved in the swim team and synchronized swimming. When we weren't training for those activities, we just played. I have a deep love of swimming because of these memories. We got grounded once for something, probably just us being annoying. I'm not sure, but we weren't supposed to have any fun. My little foster sister was just so happy all the time and finally burst out, "I know we are grounded and we are not supposed to be having any fun….BUT THIS IS SO MUCH FUN!!!". That is the enthusiasm I loved in the girls, they really did not know how to live without having fun and living up the place. I got to visit the pool which was in the middle of one of many greenways in my old neighborhood, adjacent to the tennis courts and giant maple trees again on my last trip to Oregon, and it is one of the more nostalgic places of my childhood.

I remember Christmas when we all got American Girl dolls, each one of us got a different character. Between us I remember Samantha, Kirsten, Addy, Molly, and Felicity. They were so special for us and we have that bond. I still have my own doll, and my own girls have some of the newer released dolls. I thought it was really neat that we all got gifts, and the same kind of gifts. There was not a difference between us, we all got the same kind of Christmas and were all watched over. I remember "Santa" coming by to deliver presents. We would hear the jingle bells from outside and the three younger kids would be so excited. They didn't know that it was our neighbor, Joe Price, just paying us a magical visit. They were one of the families from our church and neighborhood who really loved our foster family and showed us a lot of support. They always had giant parties at their house and we were always invited, even if we were a rambunctious large bunch of kids. They also had kids that matched our ages as well. The mom always seemed to have fresh cookies for us when we went over there. They are a big reason that we have tried to be the party house in our neighborhood. Everyone is invited, and we like to have tons of food and music. The Price family was a great example for me.

    We even went to Disneyland all together. We travelled all the way from Oregon in a van to get to Southern California. My parents promised us quarters every half an hour if we were good, but the second anyone would tattle or cry or be disruptive, the money would be taken away. It took sister #2 only once to realize she was losing money if we weren't behaving. From that point on, it was her sole mission to silence the car. Nothing got past her, because there was no way that money would be taken from her again. It worked pretty well, and we traveled in peace. I remember watching the way my parents would figure out how to deal with all of us. One of my favorite pictures from when I was a kid was all of us in front of the castle. It was so magical, and the sacrifices that my parents gave for us to be able to experience it didn't go unnoticed. When Brandon and I, twenty-five years later adopted our kids, we also made a big gesture for our family, bringing them to Disneyworld. The kids are just worth the time, effort and money to have these experiences. We had parts of the day where we would stay together doing smaller rides like Peter Pan and the teacups, then eventually when the little kids were tired, my mom would take them back to the motel so they could rest. My dad was left with the big kids, consisting of my brother and I, plus the two older foster sisters. We were able to do some of the bigger rides, like Space Mountain, Splash Mountain and Thunder Mountain Railroad. I suppose you could say that we became quite familiar with the mountain ranges of Disneyland. The electric parade was amazing, until my family crossed the street, dashing through the deafening music and swirls of bright colors, straight through the chaos without me. I was the youngest and just couldn't keep up. I don't know how long it took my dad to realize that I was separated from the herd, but I was eventually found by a cast member and escorted to the lost and found- kid version. I was fine, I don't remember freaking out too much. I could hear on the radio that they were looking for me and I was just fine just watching tv in the waiting area. We were reunited and continued on with the trip. Now if you were to bring this up with my parents, there would still be more than a few raw emotions brought up from my mom. Out of the dozens of times I have been to Disney parks, I can still pick out this special trip, and I am very grateful to my parents for the experience.

    I remember one of the biggest accomplishments of my mom's life, and we were all a part of it. It was around the year 1994 and my mom was dressed up in a black cap and gown. It was my mom's graduation from the master's program from Pacific University. She brought all seven of us to watch her graduate and see that it was a big deal. It took everything she had to graduate with so many kids, but she did it. I remember the graduating class sitting down while we were in the seats watching down on them. As they threw their caps in the air, we could see bubbles everywhere. That was pretty fun to see. I had aunts and uncles and my grandparents all there to celebrate with the family. They were curious about the foster kids, and kept a cautious eye on all of us. These are the same aunts and grandma that some 25 years or so later, came to surprise me at our own adoption party. It taught me that it was important to have the support from your family when you foster. I know that if I hadn't had the support from my family, especially parents and siblings, it would have been much harder. They went out of their way to make an effort in helping me out with my adopted girls.

The girls had many friends from church. Whether they were naturally friends, or asked to try to include them in their friendships, I'm not sure, but they had an excellent support system. Decades later, when I am able to go back and visit the very same church or visit with old friends, they still ask about the girls. Some of them had even kept in touch. I love being asked about them, because they remember that they were a real part of my family from those years.

I can't express how much sister #3 has changed my life. She was younger than me, and had so much love and excitement inside of her. Her birthday is really close to my younger sibling's birthdays, and I always try to wish her a happy birthday. I will frequently remember her excited little voice, and how cute she was when she started losing teeth. She was like a twin to my sister Mandie. They had so much energy together and loved playing with barbies. She got to have a normal six-year-old childhood, which is so important. Their minds are still so innocent and full of magic. I stayed in touch with her the most when social media became a thing when we were older. She even got to visit us in Utah when I was first married. One of my favorite stories with her is when she was trying so hard in school to read. Mandie had already started reading, and so had Andy, who was two years younger. My mom worked with her good-naturedly telling her that she just had to be patient because someday it would all click with her. One day she came running home from school and shouted "It clicked!!! My brain finally clicked!" Sure enough, just like that, she had something click in her head and she started to read. I loved celebrating the accomplishment with her. I was a proud big sister.

I learned some lessons about etiquette while they were with us. These girls loved to eat. They could out eat me any day. My parents had to set up new rules for dinnertime. Often, we would find them scooping out the food into their dishes the second they sat down at the dinner table, and even during our family prayer. I watched as my parents taught them to be patient, wait for the signal to start getting food, and even watch how many servings they were getting. We all learned along with them, that it is really important and respectful to see how much food there is and try to even it out with the rest of the people who will be eating. If one person is eating half of the food, then they needed a refresher on how much to take. My own kids are the same way. We also learned how much food was appropriate to eat in public. I remember seeing some of the girls joyfully maneuvering around the neighborhood parties with overflowing plates of cookies, brownies and chips, and seeing my parents following up quickly to intervene before too many people noticed how much food was missing. It was a lesson on being aware of what is happening around you. I teach the same lessons to my own kids.

I learned so many life lessons from my parents during this time. They taught me to have patience, even when situations aren't ideal. It is important to keep your room clean and your life organized. I spent so much time doing yard work and learning how to work hard with my dad. My mom taught us by example how to treat everyone and always be engaged in service, since we are all children of God. I also discovered that parents don't like being lied to and how important it was to be honest in your whole life, even when no one was watching. Both my mom and dad taught this to use through their own examples. I saw many consequences given out, and I was able to watch and learn from other people's mistakes, and occasionally my own. A lot of the discipline I use in my parenting I remember learning from that time. The dollar menu at Taco Bell can hold some good options when you are on the go. Stop and watch the scenery when taking drives, don't waste that time by sleeping or fighting. I also remember my sisters wanting my mom to promise them different things, and my mom refused to do it. She had learned that you don't make promises to foster children because there is no guarantee that you can keep them. They don't need any more disappointments in their lives, so she was careful to never say that she promised to do anything.

We understood that the sisters would be leaving someday. The final day got pushed back so many times, that our forecasted 6 months turned into almost two years. I remember the day we said goodbye to them. I knew we weren't supposed to be sad, because they were going home to their mom. That was the day when I learned the meaning of the word bittersweet. At the same time, being around nine years old, I had conflicting emotions of being both so happy for them and so sad at the same time. My sisters got in a van and drove away with all of their things. We had promises that we would still stay in touch. I didn't know how that would be possible though, because they were not just moving down the street. And they needed space to get used to being home again. I had watched and listened to all of the things that their mom had to get done in order for the girls to move back. It sounded like a lot of work that was very emotional and hard for all of them. Even though she was an adult, she still had many rules to follow in order to keep her family together. It was July 17th the day they drove away. My little brother Andy's birthday. Also the day 10 years later to the date that I met my soulmate, Brandon.

I remember talking on the phone several months later to get an update. They were already busy with their own lives. I reported to them that I have started taking violin lessons. I heard that my little foster sister was getting baptized. We were lucky enough to go to the baptism and see them again. I think that was the last time I remember seeing them before we moved out of Oregon to California, then eventually to Utah. I was in college when Facebook appeared. It didn't take long to reconnect with my little sister. You know how it is, the younger people are always the first onto the social media scene. I had always talked about my wonderful foster sisters, but now I had a way for them to get back into my life again. She came to visit and it was like having a cousin come and hang out. It was several year later before I friended sister #2, and then eventually sister #1. I loved catching up on their lives and all of the successes that they had had. It was not easy, they all went through their own trials over the years, and now I was getting to see who they had become because of it. They are all in the same area Back in Oregon and are still very close.

    I got to visit with two of them in 2017 for ice cream, and it was like being back home with family again. In the summer of 2018, we made the trek out to Oregon as a whole family. Brandon and I had my five kids and my parents with us. We were coming into the campsite for the first night and surprised my family with two of my foster sisters. We got to visit with them, not for very long, but long enough for my kids to get interested in our story. Later in the week we were staying at the condos at the coast in Seaside, our family's favorite place to vacation, and all three sisters were able to come stay with us. We ate food and sat around the couches with the kids on the floor, reminiscing about the old times. One of my sisters had a ten-year-old daughter, the same age as Emma. They called each other cousins, and hit it off right away. Emma was quick to come up with nicknames for her new aunties, as she called them. This was the first time that we had all been together, or seen them together since the baptism more than twenty years earlier. We got a picture of all of us, and it was like going full circle. It was emotional being all together, a family, because of my parents' one decision to foster. It is because of my experiences as a foster sister, that I truly learned the worth of people in the world. Everyone deserves to be loved. Everyone deserves a family. The impact of my fostering childhood can be seen and it is spreading. I can show that love too.

I know my foster daughters could feel it too, because this was the same week that Tabitha finally broke the news to us that she was ready to be adopted. I had been waiting for so long to hear those words, and when she said them, from the front of the ten-person bike that we were attempting (poorly) to maneuver through the small streets of Seaside, I did finally have tears come to my eyes. I had imagined the moment hundreds of times the previous year, and It was finally becoming real. She had been deciding if that is what she wanted to do for a long time, and now we finally got to hear the words. I truly believe that foster care can save lives, and I want my family and my foster sisters to know that I love them and my life has been changed because of them. In return, the joy that I see in my children's lives radiates, because of the love of foster care.

We don't foster for a Happily ever after

What comes to mind when I say the words foster care? Usually those words bring up images of sad little children dirty from being on the streets, hungry and alone. Enough negative talk! I want you to see what the words foster care mean through my eyes. Let's try to change the vision for you. Here are my fostering affirmations:

- I love that I get to be a foster parent!

- I love doing foster care!
- I love foster care!
- I love!

Now I would do foster care even if I didn't get to see the blessings from it. It would be hard, but I would still do it, for a couple of years at least. If you go into it *not* expecting to have a wonderful life changing experiences, you will be amazed when you do and you open your eyes and see the miracles. Even the teensiest, tiniest joys are miracles. If you get used to seeing life in black and white, then it makes you appreciate the color when you do finally get to experience it. Let me show you how these affirmations are unique:

1. I love that I get to be a *foster parent* who invites children into her home through foster care. I love that I am one of the people who get to minister to these young children. I get to make a difference. I am there through the hard times and the fun times. I chose this path. It could be a horrible experience, I know that. I am willing to try at least. There are some kids out there that I don't think I would be a good match with, because of my mild personality and inability to handle certain tough situations. Somehow, I was able to manage every child who came. Know when to say yes, you think you can handle it, even if it is a struggle. Know when to say no, you are not the right person for that kid. Realize this however, the caseworkers trying to place the child usually only tell you the bad things, because that is all they know. Children are not defined by the few negative things that people know about them. Children are resilient and amazing! If you aren't seeing the positive in children, then maybe it's all about your perspective. I love that I get to witness the progress they make in school and in therapy and in themselves. Seeing my biological

children learn to open up their homes and their own personal bedrooms to these new siblings is a growing experience for everyone. My home eventually become a place of solace for many people. Over time they come and feel welcome. I have grown so much by being a foster parent.

2. Why do I love *doing* foster care? I love that we have a system and structure for the little people in our society who have a need to be safe. They are not living in orphanages or working in sweatshops. They are not to live in the sewers or hid in subway tunnels. I am aware that the system doesn't always work, but when it does, these kids have a bed and a shower, and clean clothes in a warm home. It's not easy on anyone's part to get adjusted, but at least there is a place for them to go. I am a foster care advocate. I chose to be, because I think that if more people hear my story and feel, that maybe they could also open up their homes, then I have made a tiny difference in the life of another child. They get to learn how to be functioning people because of the work I do in the home. Hear my story. Talk about foster care. Talk about teaching love. Isn't that another way of saying foster care? We teach love when we show it. How wonderful is that! What if, the more love you gave, the more you got back? I don't think it works like that, but treat the world like that's the truth. Like it is the secret of life. Let it shock you.

3. I love *foster care*! Why? Because I am seeing the world in beautiful Lisa Frank colors. I can't live in black and white, it doesn't work for me. I have to rejoice in the little successes I get to experience with my kids. I get to grow my hope. Foster care gives me the opportunity to help mold and shape another person. I get to teach them about the colors I see. Foster care is basically giving the kids a safe home while the biological family gets the opportunity to work through the services the state encourages them to complete so that they can learn the skills to keep their

family safe. There are so many services that they may be offered. Some may include drug testing, therapy, peer parenting, parenting classes, in home respite programs, using the crisis interventions, taking skill building courses, behavior testing and supervised visits. Parents are not automatically shut out, generally they still get the chance to visit with the kids in a safe and secure location. The parents get the chance to grow and get help. There is somewhat of a deadline, so they are given specific instructions to help manage and complete their tasks. I know that if I were in that position, I would do everything right away and rush through the system, because I have a clear head with no addictions or major obstacles. We can't just expect the same outcome with these parents. They have a lot of struggles, and often make bad judgements. Our job as foster parents is to be on the child's team, and to be their parent's cheerleaders, if we can. It can be hard, but at least in front of the kids, they need to know you are rooting for them.

4. I *love*. I had the ability to love before I was a foster parent. I think everybody has that ability. I will say that my ability to love because of foster care has grown and expanded significantly. It's wonderful to be able to love, and I feel blessed for that capability. There is so much love in the world, and I see it every day. I am in tune to it. Even my Facebook is full of inspiring and wonderful things that are in the world. Use the Facebook algorithm in life. The more you like great or funny or wholesome or kind things, the more you will be shown those kinds of things. Some people only see the tough political negative things, because that is what they have chosen to like in the past. To be honest, my Facebook feed is primarily pictures of my friends' cute families and their adventures, with some funny animals, religious thoughts and memes that make you smile. It's positive and I enjoy being enlightened while still on social media. I also hear a ton of amazing fostering stories. It's what I have built it to be. Apply that to life. Be that person who loves everyone. Turn yourself into someone that surrounds themselves

with wonderful people who don't limit their goodness. Be the kindness in the world that you want to see. I enjoying being around the people who are the first to laugh and give hugs. I am not a great hugger. I will never be the first to offer a hug, other than to my family members. I wish I was, but I have a pretty small comfort zone. I really like surrounding myself around that kind of person though. I like being around the good. Love is a lot of things, we know what the Bible says: Love is patient. Love is not provoked. Love endures all things. Love does not brag and is not arrogant. Love believes in all things. Love is kind. Love hopes. I have found more love by being a foster parent. Or maybe it has found me.

I get asked all the time, is fostering worth it? Is it rewarding? Fostering is hard work. Being a mom is hard. That alone Is being literally the best mom you can be, the best wife, neighbor, babysitter, worker, church goer, teacher etc... while raising little people and making sure they are safe, happy and healthy. Adding foster children means you have to do all of that, but also raise other people's children that usually have been abused or neglected in some way. They are traumatized no matter what. Even coming into a good decent living family in itself is traumatic. So we grow patience. I grow more every day. We work day and night for these children. Every child is worth it. They have a whole team working to make sure they are in the right place. They have entered the court system and have a judge looking out for them. They are loved so much even if they don't know it.

The day that I adopted my daughters was one of the best days of my life, and of my family's life. I won! I got the golden prize and adopted from foster care! It was the perfect day, complete with a photo shoot and a bbq. At least a hundred people came to party with us, including a surprise visit from my grandma and two aunts. This was before the pandemic obviously. Everyone knew how happy we were because everyone was full of smiles and laughter. My oldest even had picked out her own dress for the event, and it was a light pink. When we met her, the colors of her wardrobe varied from black to grey, and on a colorful day we saw from dark blue or red. Now she can wear pink and even sport heels that are taller than anything I own. Everything was perfect that day-kind of like when you see pictures of a gorgeous destination wedding and the photos are dreamy and touched up to hide any flaws. That's what it felt like that day.

That's not why you get into fostering however. If this is your end goal when you sign up for this, then get out now. You can't make this about you. The first and foremost reason that foster care should be considered should always be to help a child. The primary goal is going to start with reunification with the birth family. I'm not saying that going home is always the best option- of course not, that would be crazy. We wouldn't clap our hands and shout for joy to send kids back home to a drug house. We are not here to lead a lamb to the slaughterhouse. Our main purpose is to care for the children until a permanent, safe, structured and loving home is ready and established. Sometimes that home turns out to be our own. There are going to be times however, that you can tell the state agency that you are only interested in adopting. This option is not as common because our biggest need in any community is going to be finding foster homes willing to take kids, especially sibling sets. All except for one time, we have always taken siblings.

Why were we so happy? What made that day so great? We get to be the ones who they call family. It really doesn't take long at all to get very attached to these kids, sometimes it is an instant connection. By the time our adoption happened, I was already willing to do anything for these girls. Now I get to be the one entrusted to lead and guide them throughout their lives. They are siblings to my kids, and they have a place in our home. Nothing will separate us, even if we go through tough things, we are still there all their journey.

One night during the hustle of dinner prep Tabitha asked, out of nowhere, if we had ever looked at someone that we had only known for a short time and felt like we had known them forever. Brandon and I smiled at each other because within a few days of knowing each other we had felt the same way. That's one of the first times I knew we were meant to be together. Then I got suspicious and asked why she was asking, fearing that at her young age she may have become infatuated with a boy. I was relieved when she said that she had just had that thought as she had just seen me a minute ago. It was a sweet experience. I tried to explain how Anne of Green Gables would have poetically interpreted that as being bosom buddies and that practically brought audible crickets to the room. Too above her head. I left it at maybe our spirits recognized each other and we were meant to be connected. We invest so much of ourselves in our biological and foster children, that it makes sense that we feel like we have known them much longer. My daughter said it did not feel like we have known each other only a year and a half. I feel the same way. This is a great benefit to fostering, the unity that can form over time.

We all have doubts when it comes to our abilities. What if I fail? You may, to be honest. You are dealing with real humans who have real emotions. Placements may fail, even adoptive placements are sometimes reversed. I am quite positive that some of my placements went home and were told so many bad things about foster care, that their memories are going to be altered based on what the parents tell them about us. It is frustrating. We had some really great times, and helped them get through some amazing obstacles, and I am sure the progress we made were reversed in the first week. I can only wish that they remember the skills that we teach them. I have never had a placement removed from us, or asked to have one removed. In that sense, I didn't fail. There are days though, when I go to bed and know that I didn't handle things correctly, or think of something too late that I should have done to alter the situation. Maybe I failed that day. You may fail, but as long as you don't give up, you are not a failure. How will you know unless you try? What if I don't really have what it takes? Then do some research. I honestly hope that reading this book may help to answer some questions about what you think you can and cannot handle. Assess your strengths, and find some people to ask. There are question and answer panels all the time, in fact I do a couple a year. I think more people are perfect for fostering and they don't even know it. You could be one of those families. If you follow your curiosity, how far are you going to make it? Just like jumping off of the mountain analogy, you won't know what you can do if you never even take a look. There is always room for change, and learning and even starting over once in a while.

I love the thought to be the change that you wish to see in the world. This is me doing my part to do just that. My goal is to change your way of thinking about foster care. Here is another reason that you may want to impact the life of a foster child. They are going to grow up and contribute to the world, with or without you. They are out there and are already a part of your own family's world. With positive influences and support systems, that could be the difference between winding up in the streets versus becoming a CEO. You never know what they are going to become, but also, you never know the impact that you may make. They already are a part of your world, you just may not have seen their impact yet. There is a man who teaches at the local middle school around here. He grew up in a horrendous situation, and lived through foster care. He was homeless and things could not have been worse in his story. He found a family that was able to take him in, and that was the first change that affected his life. He went on to join the military, and lost a leg during his service. He had enough of a strong home base that he pulled through. He got married, has children, and teaches science. He teaches because he wants to see the wonder in his student's eyes when they learn about science in their world.

Think about yourself. Were you a foster child? Or was a family member of yours one at one point? What are the differences that you may have seen in your own life? There is a pretty good percentage of foster parents in the groups that I am a part of that have been foster kids at some point. They say that they have been touched and had a good experience, so they want to pass it on. That is great, especially if you have been able to deal with your own trauma and learned how to cope and deal with the tough situations. There are so many reasons why people might want to start doing foster care. If you are interested, look into it. It could be one of the best things that you have ever done. You might be missing someone in your life that you never knew was even missing.

You've got questions? I've got answers!

Q: Do you get paid to be a foster family?

A: Not really. Yes, as in you will receive some financial assistance to help the family provide a normal family experience for the kids. You will submit proof that you are financially stable and able to care for your children that you may currently have. The extra money will help with mainly grocery bills, clothes, driving mileage and any extra needs that the child might come with, such as diaper care. These programs are aware that the average person can't just add several people to their home without assistance. It is a small set daily allowance to help offset the impact. On the other hand, I say no because this is not a paycheck. This money doesn't vary on how good of a parent you are, or how much the state likes you. There will be a little variance depending on the intensity of level of the child.

Q: How long does it take to get licensed?

A: This will depend on a few things. Every state is going to be different on the requirements that will be needed to complete the licensing. For us, we knocked it out in about two months. We had a time crunch due to changing curriculums that forced us to get it finished by traveling all through the state to get it done. Generally, it takes a few weeks to several months to get the mandatory trainings for both partners. You will both need to get the training done, so that can be the biggest hassle working around work and family schedules. There will also be a ton of paperwork and getting the home ready for licensing. I would plan on about 4-6 months on average. It took a few months to actually get our first placement.

Q: What has been an unexpected joy?

A: One thing that surprised me was how quickly the love comes for these kids. There is something that happens when you see them for the first time. You realize that they are real people that have been put into difficult situations. They just need someone to be nice to them and take care of them. Even if you don't love them yet, treat them like you do. It's easy to show love to strangers in public, this is kind of like that. Do simple acts of service, and be the blessing that God is trying to find for them. It's simple- but it's everything.

People ask what the rewards are in fostering. It's not monetary, it's not a trophy, you don't get a certificate for every kid you have helped. No one knows the struggles and pains we deal with and that we have to watch them deal with. Fostering can be a reward for us and for them. They have a safe, healthy family that will love and serve them. I love that every once in a while, I get to piggyback off of their successes, and get a glimpse of what accomplishment they must be feeling. It has little to do with me specifically, but with a child progressing successfully through life. This may all sound hypothetical, but trust me, the emotions are real. You learn to hang onto the good ones, because they can be rare.

I get joy when my kids come home with a great score on their spelling test, or when they learn a new math concept and it starts sticking in their heads. I feel joy when they come home talking about a new friend. There is joy when they start breaking down the barriers in themselves. I can feel their successes, and they are so sweet.

There is also a joy that I feel when the kids get to go back home, in the situations when it is the best thing for the kids. One of the ultimate rewards is that if I look closely enough over time, I get to see their hearts are healing. I couldn't ask for more.

Q: Do you think it's fair to your own kids to bring foster kids into your home?

A: Here is the thing about fostering, there just is no set way of doing things. Every kid is different, and so is every case. Things change day by day. When we started fostering my kids were young, just two and four at the time. I had only been a parent for four years, so I was pretty much a newbie. We felt ready however, because we were really good at communicating with each other and talking through behaviors of why people did certain things. It's a pretty good skill to have in a marriage.

We had decided early on that we would always make sure that the safety of our family came first. This means taking certain precautions that we hadn't worried about before. AS long as we all felt that it would benefit our whole family, we agreed to move forward.

Aside from normal sibling disputes, the kids were just fine and always felt safe. Most of the effects that fostering is going to have is emotional. We looked at it as a teaching example. You can't just say that you want to go good without doing something about it. Good thoughts and intentions don't cut it when you are talking about kids who need homes. We chose to take in kids and have my own children be part of the experience. We decided together that they would gain more for caring for others than they would living their lives in ignorant bliss. Sure, we would have more money if we didn't foster, and perhaps they could have been involved in sports or other hobbies earlier in life, but we taught them lessons that will last their whole lifetime. We still had adventures and amazing opportunities provided to all the kids in our home.

If it ever became an issue of will it hurt my kids physically or emotionally to have other kids in our home, we would not have done it yet. We would have waited until our own kids were grown and then started to tackle foster care. If we had found ourselves in an unsafe situation, there are resources that we know and can call any time of night. There are places that will help us and let us bring the kids so that we can all get the help that we needed.

Coming into this as a religious family helped the situation too. The core of our family's relationship is based on having enough faith to go forward with the direction that you are guided towards. We did not do this on our own, we believe that we had a Heavenly Father there with us every step of the way.

After making sure that you are prepared and ready for it, then yes, I think it is fair. We are teaching our children about humanity and how to help, love and serve others. We are teaching them that there is a world outside of our family, and we can get involved and make a difference in it. Perhaps we as a family were able to change the tiniest part of the world and make it better. If everyone lived this way, the world would be a pretty incredible place to be.

Q: What are your thoughts on fostering if you are a single parent?

A: What I love about the marriage relationship that I have, is that I have a built-in parenting buddy. When things get hard, we can tag team it and bring our slightly different parenting style to the table while still sharing the same belief system. What really works for my family is that I am able to arrange my schedule in such a way that I can be here to take care of the many meetings and appointments that need to be covered. We don't get to choose the layout of our calendar as foster parents. You have to learn to be flexible and be where they want you, when they want you. This refers to the many team meetings, school visits, therapy sessions, court appearances etc. It has been very helpful that one of us was there to keep the kids on top of everything. If I were working full time, and the sole caretaker of children, I would have a hard time handling everything. I am in awe of single parents, and have a great respect for those who are able to successfully juggle it. Although knowing my own skills and strengths, I don't know if I would do fostering while single, but it can absolutely be done. If you find yourself in this category, my advice is to be present. Parenting is a 24/7 job, and you will need a way to find balance and peace within the day. You have to find a way to take care of yourself so that you can take care of the kids. No one is asking you to be perfect, and you may wonder if you will be enough. Bolster your village and make certain that your support system is already strong and ready for your journey. When you are ready, foster away, and know I am rooting for you.

Q: Am I going to be a good enough foster parent. We don't provide a perfect home, we can provide a good home.

A: If you had to have a perfect home to become a foster family, then we would have no foster families at all! There are so many families that I admire. I watch foster moms jump from one crisis to another, sometimes succeeding wonderfully, and sometimes hanging on by the skin of their teeth. Every once in a while, I see them plummet to their foster parent death. We are all blessed with different abilities, skills, talents and training. Even those who appear to have all of the answers, didn't gain them upon receiving their fostering license in the mail (or email now days). I have gone to years of training, in addition to my bachelors in psychology, history of fostering as a child, following my parent's footsteps and partnering up with an incredible husband. All of these have helped me to where I am today, being a wonderfully, brilliantly, experienced...*good* foster mom. And that will do for me. I have had multiple foster kids tell me that they don't need anything fancy. They just need a normal life. My adopted teenager has been watching me get Christmas presents ready for months. She always looks at me like I am crazy, and asks why I need to get so many presents. All she really wanted is her favorite candy bar and she is set. She just wants to live in the moment of Christmas. She says the gifts aren't necessary, but I can tell by the look in her eyes that she loves and appreciates them. "I used to not get anything for my birthday or Christmas, I'm used to it". I get so many gifts because I want them to know that I care for them, and want them to experience the magic of the holidays, and to let them know that they are important. She sees the sacrifice that I make, and that is what means more to her. I am willing to sacrifice for my family, and you are included in that. There is a funny foster care commercial that comes to mind. A few kids are playing in the sprinklers outside their foster home when the ice cream truck goes by. Their ears perk up instantly, as would happen with most kids, and they eagerly rush to the mom to see if it is their lucky day and they get some ice cream. The mom, being a realistically logical parent, shakes her head no.

"Please, mom Please!"

"No. We are having dinner soon"

"Pleeeeease"

You can see the disappointment creeping across the children's faces. Then suddenly out of the house bursts the foster dad, barefoot and all running past the kids chasing after the ice cream truck. The kids glance at their mom's face then bolt after the dad laughing at their change of luck. It is a reminder that you don't have to be a perfect to be a perfect parent, and you are not expected to try to be perfect. Just do your best, like we tell our own children. There are thousands of children in foster care who will take you just the way you are. I just love this! We are not perfect, and the kids that come are not perfect, and that's ok. They just need someone to be there so that they can have the opportunity to have everyday experiences. My biological kids have always known what it is like for me to be there when they come home from school, and any foster kid that I have had has had the little adjustment to having a parent always there, and always present. You do not need to strive to be a perfect family, it is daunting trying to rise to a standard that high. Instead, pick some qualities and emulate those. Maybe you need to work on patience, or loving unconditionally, becoming an advocate at their school is great, and so is learning to set boundaries. There are so many ways we can be great, so find your strengths, or learn what they might be. Work on yourself and learn to be present. You will do great!

Q: How do you deal with knowing these kids are likely NOT going to be permanently in your home?

A: First of all, you will almost always start out a case with reunification and a hazy future in sight. It becomes so easy to grow attached to these kids, and I hear this all the time, "I could never foster because I would get too attached and couldn't say goodbye". That's great! This shouldn't be seen as a negative quality at all. Instead of letting that hinder your thoughts and intentions, use it! They need love and attachment. They need cheerleaders and role models. It would be so negligent on our parts if we opened up our homes but kept them at a distance. They need to be close to people and to make connections. That is a wonderful thing! If they do end up going home and never have contact with you again, they will at least remember that someone cared for them. If they go home and it is a good experience being reunited with their family, then you have been a stepping block to getting them there. We are meant to have connections, whether it is for just a few short days or they are with you a lifetime. Don't shortchange their connections to the good in the world. So my best advice is to enjoy the day that you are in. Right now. If you have a foster child, or two or three, look them in the eyes and listen to them when they talk. Take advantage of this day that you have. Look back on the days you have already had with the kids, and learn from them. If they were hard, focus on how much you have grown. If they were good, then use those memories to lighten your burden that you carry now. They need time for just you every day, so make sure to push pause for a few moments and let them take control of the conversation. As adults we get so used to our routine and micromanaging that we forget to let them take control so we can teach them some skills needed for connecting to people. I would say that more often than not, the foster kids that you get won't stay in your home forever. Make the most of every day because you really, really don't know when it will be the last.

Q: How do you help your biological kids understand that their siblings are likely only temporarily.

A: I have heard so many people step back from the prospect of fostering when they consider how their children will handle the adjustments. It can be hard for sure. Some parents worry about what may happen if you mess with the birth order of your kids. I look at it this way, my oldest daughter, Lyla, has at one time been the oldest, youngest and middle child at some time in her childhood. She is one of the most well-rounded children I have ever met. She understands that sometimes we get bumped from the bedrooms, or our place in the car. There will be times when she won't get to sit by me in church, so I have learned to adjust myself in order to help her adjust. Maybe the new kid feels like she must hang onto me at the same time that my toddler MUST sit on my lap. I find myself twisting to get in just the right position so that the little one balances delicately while I don't breath too hard, and I have my arm around the needy one, while secretly holding the hand of the child on the other side of them. As long as there are no sudden movements, every kid is content getting just the right amount of attention without knowing that I may be also be preoccupied with giving comfort to a sibling. When the foster kids go home, your family has another adjustment period. My older biological kids relish the attention that can now be more dedicated to them. "It's nice to be just the regular family again" I have heard many times. As much as they might love being a foster sibling, they notice when the family snaps back to the normal routine again and they can enjoy their space again. Once things stabilize again, which happens pretty quickly, they start mentioning how nice it would be again to have a brother or sister to share their room with. Kids are resilient. They have hearts that expand so easily that they miss their foster siblings and ask for more.

There are certain phrases that are helpful. It's good to be honest with all of the kids. When the little fosters ask when they will go home, it's best to just give them a hug and let them know that we don't know how long anyone will stay with us, but that we will love every day that they get to spend with us. "I wish I knew, because you are such an awesome kid!" is a phrase I hear myself saying a lot. It's enough to let them know that you are watching out for them, and you are okay with whatever the outcome will turn out to be. They understand the concept once you understand that your family is special because you are willing to help kids who need a safe place to live. If you were to go into a second-grade classroom and ask if they would make room in their homes for a child who was having to be taken away from their parents, they would all volunteer to give up their beds, their dinners and their special blankets, just so the kids would feel loved. Even if you were to go into a high school and ask the same question, I know that a good chunk would even be willing to give up more. Don't underestimate the amount that your kids can love. They know that they have blessed lives and are willing to share their families. It can be hard, but it can also be an amazing opportunity.

Q: Can I take foster kids on vacation with my family?

A: Absolutely in many circumstances the kids can go anywhere that your own kids can go. You will need to get permission to leave the state. I will typically bring it up casually to the caseworker and give them as much notice as possible. They will ask the biological parents their opinions and email their team to get consent. If the parents agree, then you will get it in writing for everyone to sign it. If the parents don't agree, which may happen if they don't have a trusting working relationship with you, there is still the team that can discuss it. In some cases, it can be brought through the guardian ad litem, the children's attorney, and even the judge. The only time that I did not get clearance was when we were planning our trip to Banff National Park in Canada. Even with six months of notice, we were rejected in our request. It had gone all the way up to the state level for clearance, and just didn't happen. It was very hard to leave the kids, and I don't think that it was fair. Typically, the kids will be allowed to travel with you.

Q: I don't think I could ever say goodbye to them because I would grow too attached to them. How do you do it?

A: This is a very common comment that foster parents get. Just for reference, there are a lot of parents that don't like being asked this. Sometimes you can't tell if it is a backhanded insult, or if they are being sincere. Be careful about how you word the question. This question doesn't have an affect on me, so I can answer it. Well, thanks for the compliment that I am handling it well. Sometimes I am a wreck with worry when they leave, and if I am not showing it, then way to go me. I do think about the kids that go home all the time. My kids bring them up regularly and we laugh and learn from the times we had with them. The goal is typically reunification, so always keep that in mind. It can be really hard sending them back, especially when you don't know that you have total faith in the situation. Just know that you did your best, and you have been a positive impact on their growing up. I like to think that when a child goes home, it is like a rubber band around a handful of pencils. If a pencil is removed, the rubber band is still holding the pencils together. There was a little change in the shape and location of all the pencils, but it is still held together. It is nice to have some time to recover from the changes when they go home, but there is room to sneak another pencil within the hold of the rubber band. There is room for one more, because you have already made room for one more. If you are trying to say that I have a big heart by taking the children in, then thank you. If you are trying to imply that my heart is NOT big enough, because I am willing to let the children go and then go on with the rest of my life, then you don't understand the process. I have been changed by each foster child I have ever met. I learn from them and love them.

Q: Do you feel guilty when you say no to a placement?

A: Again, it varies. We want to help every foster child, that is a given. We also have to learn our own personal limits, and what will work in our family. It was only a week or so after we adopted that I started getting calls to take two more children. Well, our house and cars were already full, and we were in the process of becoming an official family. I had to let them know that we just don't have room, and if they had a temporary placement, I could do that. I did feel bad and think of those kids for days, but the time was not right. I know that my whole family would not have agreed either. Things were still new, and we were getting used to our new normal. What really happened was that someone in the office saw that we didn't have foster kids anymore, and figured we had room for more, not realizing we had adopted. Every once in a while, we would get a call about someone who was slightly abusive and sexually reactive. We again had to say no, because we had young girls in our home, and needed to protect them. But, if the timing were right, I would have absolutely taken on that specific challenge. I have to have faith that somewhere out there, a family is waiting for them and they have the time, space and ability to take each placement. You have to know your limits and do what is best for your family. I can confidently say no to a placement, and still have my heart break for them at the same time. It's just a lesson we have to go through.

Pulling memories from Facebook

I often write about my fostering experience on Facebook. I never know if people are going to respond, or even care, but I do it anyway. Here are some of my posts from the precious years. (I want to scatter these throughout the book is possible, with a different font. All of these words come directly from my own Facebook posts.)

November 22nd 2016

Another foster care post-I know there will be a lot of them, but sometimes it's a good thing and shouldn't be taboo. I like to think that these kids are placed with a family on purpose, a family that will fight for them. This girl, by some miracle, gets to stay in her own school. That almost NEVER happens.

This morning as we are getting ready for lunches, she BEGS me to make her a home lunch-because she has never had one before and always wanted one. I asked what she usually has for breakfast and she says she doesn't ever remember having breakfast at home before. I think she will be surprised that my kids get a note in their lunch every day.

So I bring her to visit with my 1st grader's teacher, who used to be her own 1st grade teacher. The teacher sees both girls, makes the connection and bursts into tears. She says she had been fighting for this girl for years to have her be in a safe stable home. She says that she will be the sweetest girl. She went on and on for about ten minutes about how wonderful she is, the challenges she has been through, and how good our home will be for her.

My new foster daughter (I use that phrase, always, as a term of endearment. It's not a bad thing. It means they have a family that is ready to love her). -holds my little girl's hand skipping through the hallway, stopping strangers and friends telling them all they are sisters. They hug and squeal.

We see the principle in the hallway. He knows of my fostering in other schools, but was shocked when he found out this girl gets to stay here in this school. He has been fighting for her too.

I meet her teacher. She starts to cry also, saying she is finally getting what she deserves. She has been struggling the whole year, again fighting, for this girl. She catches me up on the work I need to do to get her to grade level. I'm up for the challenge.

I walk into the office to make sure the paperwork is ready to go. The secretary was so excited that she met with the caseworker last NIGHT, to set everything up. She had tears in her eyes as she expressed as she had been hurting for this girl for years. She has been fighting for her.

Foster care can bring miracles. She will thrive. She will succeed. She has new sisters and a brother. She gets a Mom and Dad who are going to fight for her rights and wellbeing. No kid should be in these situations that progress so much that every aspect of their life is suffering. Share this post if you want others to see that foster care can be a wonderful thing.

February 3rd, 2017

I get asked all the time is fostering worth it? Is it rewarding? Fostering is hard work. Being a mom is hard. That alone Is being literally the best mom you can be, the best wife, neighbor, babysitter, worker, church goer, teacher etc...while raising little people and making sure they are safe, happy and healthy. Adding a foster children means you have to do all of that, but raising other people's children that usually have been abused or neglected in some way. They are traumatized no matter what. Even coming into a good decent living family in itself is traumatic. So we grow patience. I grow more every day. We work day and night for these children. Every child is worth it. They have a whole team working to make sure they are in the right place. They have entered the court system and have a judge looking out for them. They are loved so much even if they don't know it.

We have to stop and enjoy when things go right. when My girls had a really good day yesterday. They got along the entire day, they had a special visitor take them to a breakfast (Kelsie thank you), and they even helped each other with homework willingly. Usually they are very competitive because they are so close in age. By the end of the day they were hugging and laughing all the way to bed. I told them it really makes me happy to see them like that.

On the way to the bus stop I was talking to them about how nice yesterday was and they said that they stayed up last night in their bunk beds and made a plan to have another wonderful day today. I told them that would be great. My foster daughter, who is 8, only sees the good in the world, which is a little challenging because she doesn't understand why she is with us. Or at least she can't admit out loud that things were not as they should have been in her home. She finally said, "I used to have a crack in my heart. And now it feels super glued back together." It's simple. But it's everything.

People ask what the rewards are in fostering. It's not monetary, it's not a trophy, you don't get a certificate for every kid you have helped. No one knows the struggles and pains we deal with and that we have to watch them deal with. Now this was her reward. She has a safe, healthy family that adores her. She can start putting the pieces of her heart together. I get to piggyback off and steal some of that reward for myself. This is the reward-that her heart is healing. I couldn't ask for more.

September 26th 2017

Fostering and the influence of music

Here's something cute my teenager does. I have a grand piano in my house and will often sit down and randomly play songs throughout the day. It's a little classical, popular or most often from a musical. She will often open music books to certain songs, tap me in the shoulder and point to the piano as a request. So I'll try to stop whatever I'm doing and go play for her. I don't have much of a singing voice, so it's all piano.

Whenever she has her teenage friends over, she will bring us all over to the piano so I will play for them. The songs are emotional ones and she likes to share with her friend how she is feeling through music. If Brandon is home, we elicit his voice to try to "make the teen cry", by explaining the deeper meaning behind song like "Empty Chairs at Empty Tables" or "Bring him Home". Mean, I know. But she loves it. She even watched Les Miserables with us after we played enough of the songs for her.

She is in the band at school and will have me play along with her on the piano as she practices her clarinet. I'm also the one that went on a warped tour with her to see her favorite bands. That was a really great day for us. As she reports, it was the greatest day of her life. It's nice to have a bond with music. Can pick up any instrument around her and start to play it.

When she first came over six months ago, she hid in her room and listened to music with her headphones. I was sure we wouldn't agree on the music we listened to. I was sure it was death metal. It took several months for me to convince her that she could listen to her music without the headphones. She told me this week that she was afraid I wouldn't like her at first just because of the music she listened to. Well guess what, it's almost the same stuff I listen to. I know every song on the radio, and she can name who it is and the title. On long road trips she likes to play the game where she plays a song and I have to name it. Although I may not know the name, most of the time I can sing along with the chorus.

She is one of the reasons I have been donating my time to teach foster families the piano. Often foster families, like my own, can't afford to enroll kids in any extracurricular activities, due to time and money constraints. This is my way of spreading something to foster families purely for the reason that they need opportunities to get involved and develop talents.
I want and believe that music should be a staple in every life. It is something that I find anyone can relate to and use in life. I love how it has brought me and my daughter closer.

June 1st 2017

A foster child's birthday

A statistic that I hear floating around is that children in foster care are usually in care for about 12 months- on average. That means that the majority of the time they will have the opportunity to celebrate their birthday while in foster care. Sometimes that's a good thing, sometimes it's not. And my family we just like to make a big deal of birthdays. Everyone usually receives several inexpensive (for a thrifty person like me) but fun and fitting gifts.

The first two little guys that were placed with me celebrated One of their birthdays about half of the year into the placement. His brother had only joined us a couple months prior. And talking about birthdays can be a very touchy subject in foster care land. So my instinct was to buy a gift for his brother as well. They each got pool towels of their own. And then the birthday boy received the usual presents and party and cake. It turned out that was a good idea. And their mother also had a similar idea and both boys got something similar on the birthday. When it was the brothers turn, we had actually gone to Las Vegas for the night so we had a little party in a hotel there. We are able to make them both feel special.

We had a wonderful birthday girl a year ago, and her birthday was so close to Lyla's and another cousin birthday, that were able to throw a combined party with family as well as individual parties with just us. That bouncy energetic girl enjoyed every minute.

I've had my one foster daughter (Emma) about six months, and her sister (Tabitha) followed about three months ago. Many of you saw the post about her birthday party and making her cake and how it was such a wonderful experience that she got to be spoiled that day. But the problem is, she was only spoiled by our family and her friends-not her biological family. And unfortunately, there has been manipulation and lying coming from biological family, and promises of birthday gifts have been broken. Tabitha's birthday was over two months ago, and she still hadn't received a gift from the family member. But she has been growing in so many ways and is looking at it as just a life lesson and it's affecting her in good and bad ways.

Tomorrow is Emma's birthday. And she's excited. Do you know how I know? Because she has been counting down her birthday since the day that she came with us last year. Many of you have had a chance to meet her and know how amazing both of these girls are. My life is incredibly blessed to have them here as part of my family.

Now I try to never say anything negative about the biological family, but this is kind of relevant to the point that I want to share today. The Birthday girl tomorrow will have a birthday party with her biological family and plenty of presents. It is incredibly hard on her sister to not be jealous, but it turns out this has been happening her entire life.

My oldest was able to process this information and decided that she wanted to serve and love her sister instead of focusing on jealousy issues. She then decided that she would make her sister and epic birthday cake. And I could not be more proud of her. She has been designing it for about a week and is in charge of every single detail. The younger sister who just loves to enjoy life and loves attention and being herself, has been paying attention to her older sister. She has noticed the effort that is going into her very own birthday cake. Even when she is shooed out of the kitchen by her sister, she knows it's because there is a surprise coming. This younger sister was able to step outside of herself and noticed her older sister serving her. And the more she thought about it, the more she was able to express her gratitude to her sister. Today Emma came up to Tabitha while we were working on the cake all day and handed her a gift, and it was a picture drawn just for her sister and she called it a thankful gift. Then she said to just give it to her on her birthday, and Emma said that if she waited any longer she would have tears in her eyes. So she accepted the gift and I got to witness this special moment between sisters and the love that they share for each other. I love it when love can pop out of anywhere. I wish I could post pictures of the events tomorrow. You will just have to imagine it in your minds.

June 10th 2016

I have a foster daughter who is very entertaining. She's getting ready to go on a picnic and went skipping outside yelling "I'm just going to brush my hair! I'm not even getting distracted!"....She came in a minute later and started playing the piano.

Yesterday she interrogated adult women who were dressed up as Anna and Elsa for making dumb decisions in the movie. She wears camo skirts with lacy tops and tennis shoes.

She not only dances to the beat of her own drum, she's the whole freaking percussion line.

The other day she went to 2 parks when visiting her dad. When I went to pick her up I asked what she wanted to do because she was feeling bummed out. Her answer? Go to the park! So we did. Then she came home, ran in the sprinklers and had Popsicles. She is a bubble of pure energy. We run into people she knows all over town, I lost count after about 30 people.

We are having such a blast with her, after 13 foster care kids, she's the first girl. We've been missing out!

Just thought I would share.

December 29th 2017

Over the Christmas break my 13-year-old foster daughter was fiddling with my Family Tree app and we discovered that we are related. I am related to both their step grandpa and their actual grandpa down the line. My other girls somehow caught on to all the excitement and just found out they are "cousins". They are running around the house screaming.

October 25th 2017

Confession: we are in the middle of court hearings happening every few weeks with our case. This will likely continue for a few months. I tend to get anxious the closer they are. To help alleviate stress, I go through YouTube and watch Judge Judy. It makes me feel better. I like seeing a judge get after those who are needed a stern talking to, and pretend that my judge does the same. I love our judge, and trust his judgement. But it is refreshing to see justice happening in A few minutes rather than the situations that really occur in fostering timelines.

December 22nd 2018

We had a random act of kindness today. I took our foster daughter to the dentist last week. He was inquiring about her medical history. He had been her doctor through all the years, and was there during her cancer years. The whole office knows her and makes sure to come visit with her. A dental hygienist asked what she wanted for Christmas, and she named off a toy that I knew we wouldn't be able to get her. This was the first I had heard of it, and didn't have it in our budget. He began asking about her nutrition, and she said she only gets fruits and vegetables when she is in our home. When she came to live with me, she only had a couple items of clothing and a single can of peaches. She told him about the peaches and she said she had to sneak them from the homeless people that lived in her home because that was the only food in the house. It's so heartbreaking to hear of her not so long ago past. She is extremely resilient and special. Fast forward to tonight and the dentist himself drives through the ice and snow to hand deliver the special gift that she had been wishing for. He was so touched by her sweet spirit, and in turn we were touched by his. I love that the spirit of Christ, or as some call the spirit of Christmas, can be felt and experienced. This act of kindness will always be remembered.

August 6th 2017

Today my oldest three girls bore their testimony in church. One was a standard kids one. One was talking about how much girls camp meant and the spiritual experiences she had. And the last talked about...I don't even know how to explain it. There was talk of touching a buffalo (which we didn't actually do. And it was a cow, not a buffalo). She talked of fish that stopped moving to stare at us. And how everyone was staring at her sister because she is so pretty. And how she can shade with pen on her artwork. Needless to say, I was in tears from laughter and not being able to control the moment. She just went on and on. And on. Eventually I heard a lot more laughter. I tried to signal for her to come down but she didn't look at me. In the end, it all came from the heart. I'm still proud that they all can get up there and say what's in their hearts.

November 21st 2016

For the past couple weeks I have had the feeling that I need to prepare for a little girl to come into my home pretty quick. Whenever I am about to get a placement, I can almost always tell you that I have had the feelings and guessed exactly the age and gender of the kids coming. Then I just wait for the call. Just call it instinct I guess. Not a boy, not a sibling group, just a Single girl.

Well, guess what call I got today? She will be here with us tonight. I am so excited to have her, because I've been waiting for her. She even gets to stay in the same school and go to school with her new little soon to be foster sister.

March 16th 2017

Just when things settle down and we get in a good groove with being parents to four kids, we have made the very difficult decision to foster one more. Many of you local ones will know her, and know how much she needs a good family to help her. This will by far be one of the hardest decisions we have ever made. It will also be the hardest placement we will ever have. We are nervous, but faith will keep us going. We have long term goals in mind, but she is not happy to be with us. She will be joining her sister, who many have come to learn about and love in the last few months that she has been with us.

What we need now is support from those around us-and lots of advice. Feel free to message me when you think of any good advice that will help. Of course, everything is confidential, but I still need some tips. It's funny because when we started fostering a few years ago, we agreed the ages 0-4 would be best for our family. I think the majority of families say that at first. Well that requirement gets thrown out the window pretty quick when you put faces to names. So, this month, in order to keep family and siblings together, we become parents to a teenager. Insert panic face.

I have talked to a lot of people that know her from school and they say she isn't nice to them, but you can't even imagine the trauma that she has been through. It will be a slow process and trusting us or anyone else will not come easy for her. Try to encourage her schoolmates, if they are your kids, to smile or gently approach her in kind ways. She is very scared, but has a big heart.

I will also need to start using people to watch my own kids occasionally so I can visit schools and the many appointments that we have. If I have any helpers during the day, or teenagers that want to help out in the evenings, please message me. Most of the appointments I will have to go to will not be appropriate for little kids to come to, but I don't really know where to take my kids. This will be a very time-consuming time in the next few months. I'm hoping things will settle down in the summer.

Wish us luck and bring chocolate! Just kidding. Kind of.

March 11th 2016

There are times when being a foster family becomes really rewarding. Sometimes they are few and far in between, and you have to stop and enjoy the memories you're making. Tonight I was playing the piano and the kids were making crepes in the kitchen with Brandon, it's one of their favorite comfort meals. And they would randomly run into the other room and start dancing to music. After we had dinner one of the boys organized a talent show and put it on for us. It started with the oldest announcing the lineup of the show. First was our neighbor who is Stetsons age, he came out showing us his karate moves. Then Stetson showed us his Thomas trains. Lyla was next up playing some songs that she had learned earlier today. She had wanted me to teach her piano songs to her. While doing that, she asked if I would write the songs down on music notes so she could learn that way. So that was a special moment today.

Then Brandon Did push-ups while we counted and cheered him on. The finale was the foster kids singing "See you Again", the song from the furious seven movie. They even take turns with the chorus and the rapping. That song is pretty emotional, and I loved seeing them vulnerable.

Then we watched Earth to Echo, a movie they had picked out and wanted us to watch, and it turns out one of the characters is a foster kid too. They were able to relate to it in that way. Anyway, long explanation of our night, but I just wanted to share a memory, or a glimpse into our fostering journey. These are amazing kids and they have quickly become a part of our family, even if it is just for a short time.

October 7th 2015

The last few weeks have been very frustrating because our placements have been acting out. The problem is their birth mom told them an exact date that they might be going home several weeks from now. That date isn't set for sure and it's causing a lot of anxiety in them. I'm Not sure why the mom told them, she probably thought they would be excited without knowing the consequences on our end. Yesterday one of them even said that we treat our own children better than them and it was frustrating for a few hours. But today I come out and he had drawn a little picture and left it on the table. It's hard stuff that they have to go through, I wish this was easier on them. But hopefully this is a sign that they're trying to process it in a good way.

November 4th 2016

Here is one of our many fun projects we have done in the last month. I chose this quote so as my kids grow up, especially my biological and foster daughters, they will have this as one of their core memories and values. It is from the newest Cinderella movie. It's one of those quotes you hear and think, wow, I need to remember that. We have been building and painting furniture as our newest hobby. The quote says:

"I want to tell you a secret that will see you through all the trials that life can offer: have courage and be kind. Where there is kindness, there is goodness. And where there is goodness there is magic. "

And as we made it, we decided to add just a hint of sparkle. So little you have to really look for it. In fact, it took Lyla three days to notice it was there. Just like a little hint of magic right before your eyes.

April 20, 2015

I had given one of my foster boys the assignment tonight to create his own chore chart. When I checked it out, he had written the phrases "I rock!!!" And "I am strong!"
I just think that it's amazing that he can say that about himself. If only you know what these boys have been through, this would amaze you. What good can you say about yourself?

June 8th 2015

Happy birthday to my oldest Foster boy. He's just great and loves being nine. I can't post pictures so just imagine a bunch of happy kids running around in a sprinkler and getting smashed with water balloons.

April 15th 2015

Sometimes doing foster care means counting all your ducklings every time you leave or enter a room in public. Other times it's like playing Chinese checkers with the sleeping arrangements, making sure the correct siblings and genders wind up in the correct places. The last couple months it means dashing to the whimpering baby in the middle of the night so the princess won't wake up the other princes and princesses. Nights like tonight, you get one kid to sleep at ten o'clock then make the rounds over and over again until they are all sound asleep. Then there is the weekly movie night: a new movie, fresh popped popcorn with cinnamon coconut oil and hot cocoa on this stormy night.

And it brings a great comfort to know we can provide a safe, fun and love-filled environment for kids. After all, as it says on the back of my license plate holder, "Children need families too".

August 3rd 2017

Fostering post: expressing the loss from suicide through art

There is a framed piece of art hanging on my wall. I think it's beautiful. I didn't do it. If this was my art project, I would have done some other direction and it would be totally different. But this is the truest form of art. It has meaning and it has a purpose. Do you know who DID do it? One of my favorite people in the whole world. My daughter, she is my foster daughter, but still my daughter. Here is the story.

The Utah Foster Care Foundation came up with this idea to engage teenage foster children and I think it was brilliant. They partnered with the Southwest Wildlife Foundation and did an art contest at the last campfire concert up the canyon, specifically for teenagers. A few weeks prior, we got to take the family to release three baby falcons into the wild, another activity for the teens. It was here they announced the art contest. Genius, seriously. Thank you to all of those who worked to make this happen, it really was a great way to involve my whole family. Plus, we got to listen to a concert about the history of how country western music evolved.

The theme for this art contest was "Take flight". After wrestling with this for a few weeks, my daughter was undecided. Let me tell you about my daughter. She has been through an amazing amount of traumatic events that could have crushed her. But she has managed to grow wings and soar. She is amazing and she is strong. Her inspiration and what kept her going through the darkest days of her life is music. She is a clarinet player, and has been able to connect to music, which is one thing that has helped save her life. Shortly before the art contest, she heard the news of Chester Bennington, the musician from Linkin Park, and his passing. She was shocked and shaken. She was finally able to come up with a theme for her art. Here is her project, a memoir to Chester Bennington, who died from suicide. This has helped her cope with the loss. Teens her age are surrounded by so much darkness and hate and an alarming rate of suicides. It is devastating how much suicide is a part of her middle school culture. If you have middle school or high school age kids, TALK TO THEM. I guarantee you that they are surrounded by it. This is why this art is so amazing. It's not just art. It MEANS something. One of her greatest fears is taking flight too soon.

She did the hot air balloon by shading with pen. She is amazing. She also made every bird unique. They represent someone in her life who has taken flight too soon. She would love to have many people see this art and has asked me to ask friends to share it. This is in no way glorifying suicide, quite the opposite. It's an expression of something that she feels inside of her soul.

"In memory of Chester Bennington and all those who took flight too soon. Way too many. May his soul rest easy upon the sky."

June 3rd 2016

This week we had two teenage foster boys and a six-year-old foster daughter. The six-year-old and my five-year-old daughter out-ate the boys every meal. I was preparing for massive meals and tons of cooking for our family of 8, but the two girls dominated hands down.

March 7th 2017

Living in my foster world:

I took the kids shopping at Ross tonight. All five of them. (It's so weird I can say that now). It took quite a long time and some of the kids were getting restless. My 8-year-old was super antsy and hyper. To distract her I told her to go somewhere and give a compliment to someone. She came back about ten minutes later, and said she couldn't find anyone to trick. I then explained in horror what a compliment meant. She went to remedy the situation. She spent the rest of the time going up to every stranger and telling them one or two compliments. Most people were taken by surprise. She would just tell them they looked beautiful, or that they were nice, or some other observation. The store has been open for only half a week and they are getting their glitches worked out. The customer beside us was yelling at a cashier for some item the store couldn't return because of a receipt error. Now my girl didn't notice all of this was happening because she quite enjoys living in la la land. She was flitting around like the social butterfly she is. My 12-year-old was getting anxious because of the confrontation. As we were leaving, the eight-year-old ran back into the store to give the sad cashier one last compliment she told her she was doing a great job, then she ran out of the store. This is one thing I love about my foster daughter. She can go up to anyone and give a compliment. That is a gift many of us could work on. And who knows what difference she could have made to the cashier who had a hard night. I know the customer has been yelling at her for half an hour, I imagine that the random kindness of a stranger could have made her feel a little better. Just something to think about.

October 16th 2017

I made my teenager foster daughter proud when I was blasting My Chemical Romance while cooking. She made me proud while she quoted Boy Meets World in court to the judge today.

May 31st 2018

This week I got to take my five kids to Oregon where I am from. Two of them are my foster (almost adopted) kids. One of the coolest things of this whole trip was being able to introduce them to my foster sisters growing up. It took a whole minute for them to have nicknames and call them aunties. One of them has a daughter and so we dubbed them foster cousins. We got to play in the pool, have a sleepover, and pick up shells on the beach. We got some pictures of all of us together. Still feels like family. The oldest sister and my oldest daughter went to the beach where they found no less than 20 perfect sand dollars. When we broke one open, we found a star inside. This trip has been full of great memories.

Gotcha Day

June 25th 2018 could not come fast enough. That date is our family's birthday, our Gotcha day. It took a lot of work for us to get there, and here is a general glimpse at the foster journey.

There is a long process getting to adoption day when you are involved in foster care. The bulk of waiting is the reunification process. On average, children are in care in Utah for 12 months. Everyone is encouraging the biological parents to get the necessary requirements completed. Usually this entails therapy, drug tests, getting and keeping a job, finding stable housing, having a reliable car or transportation and completing mandated parenting courses just to name a few. It sounds easy, but there is a lot of pressure to complete these things in a timely manner. More pressure is added when you have your frequent meetings with the caseworker and attorney. Everything in your life seems to be made public, and there is very little privacy. We meet with the parents at the quarterly team meetings and see them at court. We also generally have weekly visit where we drop off the children to see their parents.

It is stressful seeing the parents for everyone involved. The children are torn between the foster parents and the biological parents. Who are they supposed to love? Who do they sit by? I always encouraged them to sit by their parents if they have a good relationship. Sometimes when they are older, they don't want to even be in the same room as them, which makes it a very awkward situation. Things can get very emotional during these meetings. If you walk into the DCFS building, you will often see a security guard waiting in the lobby. It's not only the parents that get worked up. I have seen multiple cases where there is a lot of family invited, and they all have opinions. Loud ones. My job is to weigh in on the progress that the kids have done, and show how they are adjusting to the home, school and therapy. I don't say much else. If I have concerns about the family, I bring it up to the caseworker in private. Their family already sees me as the enemy, that I don't need to make it worse.

Court is another dreaded thing, for us and for the kid's family. Their faults are being dragged up and presented legally in front of everyone. There are so many hearings. At a minimum they happen every three months, but as the case gets going, it is every couple of weeks. I can visibly see the tension of the parents. They often drink a lot of water and are shaky. Most of the things that are presented from the judge and caseworker and attorneys are above their head, and they don't understand all of the legal jargon. Their attorney has to lean in to whisper what is being said. There is so much sadness on the parent's faces when things are not looking up for them. If the kids are a certain age they get to come into the courtroom. Some of them enjoy the process because they have hope, and others dread showing up.

After the initial year that the parents get in order to turn things around, the judge finally determines if an extension is in order, or if it is time to close reunification services. An extension puts another court date three months out, or so, on the calendar. There is only an extension if the judge thinks that the parents may make reasonable progress to their goals in that time. So much of foster care is just a big waiting game, and a very stressful one. Eventually the case either ends up in reunification or it is time to move onto mediation. This is when the parents meet with the caseworker, a mediator and attorneys privately to see if they can come up with a plan without having to take it to trial. Sometimes the parents will relinquish rights at this point, and sometimes the trial is in order. The benefit of relinquishing your own rights, is that you are not forced to have your rights terminated. It is a little less harsh for them, and also if they have children in the future, the rights for them are not automatically terminated. If your rights are terminated, you lose the privilege to parent any kids. I believe that if the situation progresses to the extent that you know that the kids will not be in your care, because of the choices you have made, then relinquishing is a very brave choice to make. My job is to always root for the child, and even when I know that they are safer and happier with me, it is still so heartbreaking to end the case. The tension at court is to thick and there is a heaviness there.

    I fight for these children. Not to keep them, but to make sure that they are in the place that will be the best for them. Most of them have gone back home, which is great for them. I don't have to feel the sadness when they finally get to be with their parents. The biological parents also fight for them, but they fight that they get to come home, because they think that is always the best situation. They love them, no matter if they lost control and have made so many choices that would seem otherwise. I know of the love of a parent for their babies, and it is no different for them. The foster kids don't always see this however. I have seen so many of them take the blame of the parents onto themselves. They truly believe they are not wanted or loved. It takes a lot of work on our end to help repair that damage. Once they realize that it is not their fault that they are in care, they can start to move on. Relinquishing or termination can entice a wide range of emotions in the kids. One of my kids just shrugged and said ok. Another one was both happy and sad at the same time.

Our case was more complicated because the girls had two different dads, who were not in the picture. They had to be tracked down to go through the court process as well. It was a long procedure, because one of them was not even the dad, just a random person on the birth certificate. He was in prison too, which added months of hassle to the case. He still believes that he is the dad, which we know is not the case, because of the AncestoryDNA test. Their nationalities are not even close. The other dad we actually found and located a few months after the adoption. We are working on developing that relationship.

It took over a year and a half to get to the point of finally heading towards adoption. As soon as the permanency goal was officially switched to adoption, we had our attorney on the phone within minutes. We were sent to read the green binders, which contained all of the information on the case that is highly confidential. We set up subsidy meetings, and had multiple post adopt workers come to our home to get us ready. Our only hiccup was that our oldest daughter had not decided yet if she wanted to be adopted at all. We were told to proceed with the case as if we were going to adopt her. The other option was guardianship, which took me many months to accept. My fear was that if she had chosen guardianship, that she would eventually leave and no longer want to be a part of the family. We would just be another loose stepping stone for her. This concept was actually very hard for me. I spent weeks crying when no one was around and there were days I didn't want to get out of bed. I couldn't say anything to her, because I didn't want to influence her to change her mind out of guilt. The not knowing went on for at least six months, until just three weeks before the adoption date. It was such a relief that she was choosing our family to be hers officially. Even if she doesn't call me mom. It was another lesson of patience, love and faith.

We went shopping months before Gotcha day. We weren't allowed to say the word adoption because it was like a swear word for one of my kids. So we call it Gotcha. We decided that we were going to celebrate, and make it a family day, one that we would celebrate every year. We went out on a beautiful spring day to Salt Lake City, which had so much more shopping options, and had our own shopping spree. The three younger girls got matching butterfly dresses, and got to pick their own shoes, unique to their personality. I chose a lace shirt and a choral skirt that I could wear with a green jacket (although that day we had a wardrobe malfunction, so I had a choral jacket instead.) We found a peach dress and light pink heels for Tabitha, both colors were a first for her, and she rocked them beautifully. I found an adorable suit for Stetson that fit the color scheme perfectly and a tie for Brandon. My parents also had matching clothes of their own.

We had been talking about our Gotcha trip for months, the biggest surprise my whole family had ever had to keep from my kids. Everyone was involved in it. All of my siblings and their kids and my parents were coming on the trip as well. As a stress reliever, my kids would spend weeks guessing where we would be going. They were always fishing for hints. I would tell them to pack for skiing, a day at the beach, maybe even a trip to the moon. It would drive them crazy! Several times they actually guessed it, and I had to hide my smile so they couldn't call my bluff. Once time Emma asked if we were going to Candyland, and I said yes. She ran outside and yelled to everyone "We're going to Disneyworld!!!" I had to run out there and tell the kids that she was trying to trick them.

With the weeks coming up to the adoption, we decided that we would take advantage of the summer atmosphere and throw a Gotcha day bar-b-que. We only had about two weeks from the day that they told us the adoption date until the big day. With the assistance from group texting and Facebook, we had a party lined up in no time. About a week before the big day, we were walking around our property and were trying to figure out how we would seat people. We couldn't afford much because we were out of money for the month. Since renting tables and chair wouldn't work, so we decided to use our crafty brains and build picnic tables. We managed to use logs and a few boards to make six tables. We painted them red to match our firepit pergola. We also decided that we could tear out of our fences and a dead tree and open up our park to make it more of an open concept. We moved the bbq Traeger into the park and built two serving tables. We even had woodchips donated by a new local tree trimming business. We worked on the park until the night before, and we were finally ready.

The day finally came. We had waited for so long and we were so excited. I had lined up someone to come help us do out hair and makeup, and they cancelled that morning. We had another friend come over to get us ready. We made sure the girls who had tall high heels had spare shoes as we were headed out to our photo shoot. My friend Anna kindly offered to do our photography. We were all color coordinated, probably for the fist and last time. I had not even let the kids wear their sh oes so that they had no scuff marks on them. Our hair was curled and the girls all had flower crowns. The pictures were so fun. We were finally getting pictures of us together, which was rare because usually I am the one behind the camera. They were done perfectly and the finished result was like Christmas to me. I love how the photographer was able to capture the essence of the whole family. The goofiness of the kids and their own personalities comes out perfectly in each picture. It's a perfect reminder of our Gotcha day. When we finally finished our photo shoot and had about 40 minutes until we were due in court.

All of our nerves from the anticipation were driving us crazy, so we thought that called for a Dairy Queen trip. We all carefully ate over the table making sure that not even a single drop got on the brand-new clothes. I left my family there, and took the adoptees to visit with their guardian ad litem one last time. When we were done we walked next door to the courthouse. It was finally happening! We went through the metal detectors and entered the courtroom lobby to find family and friends already waiting for us. The girls were just bouncing with anticipation. The adoption hearing was pretty basic. It took about half an hour and our judge asked all of the legal questions. We had to swear in and witness before everyone that we were going to take care of the girls for the rest of their lives. My youngest, Adeline who was 2 ½ at the time, spent the whole time running back and forth between us and the people in the seated area. She finally went under the table and for a moment of comic relief, announced that she had a poopy diaper. Many times. We were all trying to keep a straight face hoping the judge wouldn't notice. It was nice to have a little moment of laughter. He asked the girls what they were changing their names to, and recorded them. When the judge finally announced that the adoption was final, I heard Emma squeal with excitement. We were all smiles, and the girls got to pick out stuffed animals that they got to 'adopt' that day. They held them as we got in to get a picture with the judge. This was a new judge, and he mentioned how he doesn't get many court hearings that are this happy.

After we left the glass doors of the courthouse, we said our goodbyes to everyone who came. We lingered with my parents and the girls' aunt's family. We found a Monarch butterfly that landed on one of the butterfly dresses. My kids took it as a magical gift for their special day. It even came to our lunch at a Chinese restaurant. We splurged and were full by the time we were done. The rest of the day we got ready for the Gotcha bbq. And people started arriving! They kept coming. The whole neighborhood seemed to be there, and we had so much food that we ran out of table space. Teachers came from school, and other foster families came to support us. There were people there that I hadn't seen for so long. People were gathered around the picnic tables with guitars and ukuleles. There was a dance party in the backyard, and the swings around the firepit were always full. It was one of the most touching sights to see all of the people that took time out of their days to celebrate our family. I know that we were all just glowing. I had written a speech, because Tabitha asked if I would put some of my feelings into words. I had a microphone, and said the things from my heart. When I was done, Brandon sang a song he had re-written for them, to the tune of Hallelujah.

When I finally gathered all of my rambunctious kids, we let them open the family gifts. They ripped through the boxes and took out a canvas of the Disney castle, the Gotcha date and a photo album of Florida that had been lying around the house. I had bought it a few months earlier and told them that we would need it for our Florida family. Tricky tricky. They cheered and screamed as they put the pieces together. One month from that date we would be on a plane to Disneyworld and Harry Potter world. As they unwrapped the gifts, it all became so clear, that we did this for real and we had made it to the finish line. It took my breath away for a minute. When it got dark, we set up the movie Annie in the backyard and our last guests left at midnight. It was truly a magical day.

The following month was another long waiting game. We spent the time sewing Disney and Harry Potter clothes so they kids could go to the parks in themed clothes. It gave me something to do while we waited for our trip. We also had a Harry Potter marathon and watched every movie, a time-consuming feat, but we did it. Our Gotcha vacation was everything we could have imagined. It was July so the weather could be described as wearing a sweater while swimming through hot soup. Still, it was so magical for the kids. Harry Potter world won the prize for the most fun adventure of the week. We went with the entire family, many of who are big fans of the series. We even got to bring my niece and nephew and introduce them to the story. They must have had a good time, because they were Harry Potter characters for Halloween. We were walking and passed the night bus from the movies. We posed with the shrunken head while it was talking about us and even mentioned us by name. It was talking about adoption and the kids could not stop laughing. We had saved up for butterbeer for the entire family, and the older four kids got wands. We had adoption pins on our clothes, and Emma got to be picked to have an Ollivander wand pick her in the shop. We rode on the train and got to explore the Hogwarts castle. We even got drenched from an actual monsoon. As we ducked into the bathrooms to hide from the weather and could hear moaning Myrtle keeping us company. While in the line of the first actual ride that we got to go on, a worker saw us and was so excited to see our pins. She told us to wait and came back with 30 line skipper passes. She was touched that we would travel across the country to celebrate our adoption, because she was also adopted. It made our whole day, and because of the passes we were able to get into a couple more rides. At the end of the day we rushed to a Gringotts ride before the park closed. After waiting in line for the more part of an hour, we finally got on. As we were departing the ride, another worker stopped us and told us that she had also saw our pins. She told us that we needed to ride again, which we were so happy to hear. She hugged Tabitha when she found out that we had adopted a teenager. As the ride took off again, she yelled out "and remember, Harry Potter was adopted too!".

We spent the rest of the week visiting some other parks in the area, including Magic Kingdom, Animal Kingdom, and Epcot. We made memories that will always stay with us. As we were leaving Epcot, Emma was watching the light show on the big Epcot ball. Her eyes had tears in them and she said that this was one of the best days of her life. I got a picture of her watching the ball as the lights reflected onto her face as I told her that this magic was because of her. Then she hugged me. It's moments like this that remind us that every kid is worth it, and deserves a loving family. Another highlight was when we went to the Magic Kingdom and got to meet Merida. Emma chose to add this name to her middle name, and she talked for weeks about meeting her Disney princess so she could tell her all about her story. Nearing the end of the day, we saw the line for Merida. It was a long line, but we made it through. Having Merida meet Emma and Tabitha was so special. She stopped to give us individual attention and talk about why adoption is so important. Emma told her that she was brave because she made it through cancer and foster care, and that is why she chose the name Merida. She responded in her thick Scottish accent, "I've never heard anything more wonderful in my life! You know, the name Merida not only means brave, but also honorable as well. I know that with your new family you are going to live up to that name. Your addition to your new clan makes me so proud." It was such a special moment, and the picture of that meeting hangs on our wall, along with Emma's giant smile. The whole week was so special, and I am so grateful for my family sacrificing their time and money to come celebrate with us. We even got to see cousin baby Jasmine blessed that weekend. When nothing is as important as family, our adventure was able to solidify our connections. As we were leaving the Orlando airport, Stetson asked if we could adopt a twin for him, so that he wasn't the only boy anymore. All of the other kids got on board thinking they could trick us into another epic Disney and Universal vacation again. Someday, I empty promised, we'll see.

Now that we have made it through the adoption process, I am just blown away at the love and progress that they girls have brought to our family. A few months later we were sealed in the LDS temple, a religious ceremony that unites us spiritually as well. My life has forever been changed by adopting from foster care. There are more people in our family and the love has multiplied.

Gotcha Day Speech

Here are the words that my girls got to hear from me that night they were adopted:

Tabitha and Emma,

Today is your adoption day. It was just perfect and I will always remember it. As Valerie Harper says: However motherhood comes to you, it's a miracle. This whole process has been nothing short of a miracle. The timing was truly in God's hands. If it were up to me, I would have signed the adoption papers the day that I met the girls. In fact, when I found out that there was a girl who was waiting for a home right before thanksgiving two years ago, I tried to contact DCFS myself because I felt so strongly that I wanted to see if this girl could come spend thanksgiving with us. I couldn't get in touch with the right people, so I was starting to think that maybe they were going to find another home for her. I had a baby less than one at the time, so I had told the office that I didn't want long term placements since we were still adjusting to a life with three kids. You can't even imagine my relief when I was the one who was the first one they called. They told me that this would be a long-term placement, and my heart so was happy to hear that. This was on Brandon's birthday, so his present was a new daughter who was happily playing pie face and eating pizza and cake with us that night. It was one of those nights. You know the kind. Like day, only darker. She adjusted to the family instantly. We soon learned that she had a sister, so we were quick to invite her to do activities with us. She was less than thrilled at the time, because we weren't her family, and let's face it, trauma sucks. It was on my birthday months later that I got the call that they wanted to place her with us. Three days later on my mom's birthday she was with us. This was the biggest leap of faith that we have ever taken. It has taught me that when God wants you to do something that requires a lot of faith, then the reward is going to be something you can't even fathom. I believe in love like I believe in God. You can't touch it, you can't see it, but you can feel the essence all around you. I have learned that I am not the rescuer, these girls are. I have a reminder hanging in our home about the magic that can come when one is kind and has courage.

As I was thinking of what to say, I wanted to give some advice. You girls are going to find things are hard on your life, and you will feel all alone, but you are never going to be alone again. Show kindness and compassion to everyone around you, because you are not going to know the battle that they are fighting. One thing I learned from Emma was that you can't blend in when you were born to stand out. She has a fierce personality. She adds color to our family. She is a cancer survivor and her spirit teaches me to be brave which is why today she added the name Merida to her middle name. Both of these girls are going to do wonders in their lives. And in mine. Brandon has been an amazing partner in all of this. He took that leap of faith to start fostering with me. He is gentle, kind and a very hard worker.

You don't have to be blood to be family. If you let people's perception of you dictate your behavior, then you'll never grow as a person. Life's tough. If there is one person who hasn't stopped growing since the day I met her, it is Tabi. She radiates happiness and love. I get stopped almost every day by people who just want to tell me how wonderful she is, and that they love the person that she's become. I am very impressed with the solid good choices she has made. She has become someone in school that can excel and is super talented. I think somehow she inherited our musical genes. At 14, she is already working in an amazing job that provides lunches for kids during the summer. She is the first to jump in the freezing water on canyoneering trips, and can make people cry at girl's camp with her profound testimony. She spends time trying to help her friends feel better and know they are loved, even when they don't return the favor. One of the reasons that she has excelled so much was because of the love from her youth leaders. They stepped in and filled in where I was lacking. Every little thing that they have done for her was noticed. I don't know if we would be here if it weren't for the support that both girls received from our family and church.

We are still going to make mistakes, we will be able to get through any trial with the help from the family and the friends you made while you were on this journey. I truly believe that this is where you are meant to be. You have come the distance to find yourself in our home. You guys have made it through some horrific circumstances, and you have made it through foster care successfully. You will be an inspiration to others and you finally have your hero's welcome in our arms. You can't imagine the love a mother has for her children. I always knew that adopted moms loved their children, but I never knew that the love was the same as if they were your own biologically. And I love that realization. I have fought long and hard for you to have a normal childhood. And I will continue fighting for you so that you know how to become strong in this world. I can't wait to see what adventures you have in store, because I know you will soar. I am going to be a mama bear. One that sees you through everything. Protecting you, guiding you and ready to take action for your rights.

A child born to another woman calls me mom. The depth of the tragedy and the magnitude of the privilege are not lost on me. And finally, as Mother Teresa beautifully said, "Do you want to do something beautiful for god? There is a person who needs you. This is your chance".

Love you both forever!

-Love, Mom

References

Annie is a 2014 American musical comedy-drama film directed by Will Gluck, produced by Village Roadshow Pictures and Will Smith's Overbrook Entertainment and released by Sony Pictures' Columbia Pictures.

Quotes and thoughts from Disney's Lilo and Stitch 2002 American animated adventure science fiction comedy-drama[2] film produced by Walt Disney Feature Animation and released by Walt Disney Pictures.

Foster care commercial: Ad council Adoptuskids. YouTube video found at Ad Council - Adopt US Kids_Ice Cream_30.mov

L.R. Knost   When little people are overwhelmed by big emotions, it is our job to share our calm, not join their chaos. The Gottman Institute

Harlow's experiement: Harlow HF, Dodsworth RO, Harlow MK. "Total social isolation in monkeys," *Proc Natl Acad Sci U S A*. 1965.

Quote by Erin Hanson: (I couldn't locate the actual poem to cite it officially)

"There is freedom waiting for you, on the breezes of the sky, and you ask, 'What if I fall?'

Oh, but my darling, what if you fly?"

Johnny Lingo references. No actual quotes used, just the concept.

The film is licensed by Covenant Communications, and is sold on DVD by BYU's Creative Works Office. The 1969 short film Johnny Lingo that is based on a story by Patricia McGerr.

Valerie Harper quote. Actress and adoptive mom: Direct quote "However motherhood comes to you, it's a miracle"

 Mother Teresa direct quote: "Do you want to do something beautiful for god? There is a person who needs you. This is your chance."

Jody Landers: A child born to another woman calls me mom. The depth of the tragedy and the magnitude of the privilege are not lost on me.

Cinderella "I want to tell you a secret that will see you through all the trials that life can offer: have courage and be kind. Where there is kindness, there is goodness. And where there is goodness there is magic. " Director:

Kenneth Branagh

Writers:

Chris Weitz (screenplay by), Charles Perrault (story) 2015

Made in the USA
Columbia, SC
26 September 2021